Answers for
an Enquiring Mind

Spiritual Teachings from White Feather
given through the mediumship of
Robert Goodwin

Best wishes
Robert Goodwin

Compiled and edited by
Robert Goodwin & Amanda Terrado

Answers for an Enquiring Mind

ISBN 0 9535210 1 X

Other White Feather Publications
Truth From the White Brotherhood

First published 1998
Available from Psychic Press, The Coach House
Stansted Hall, Stansted, Essex CM24 8UD

The Golden Thread

First published 1999
Available from R.A. Associates, Grange Court, Rushall
Walsall, WS4 1PH

Visit the White Feather Website:
http://web.ukonline.co.uk/mandrob

E-mail: whitefeather@bluecom.net
or: mandrob@ukonline.co.uk

Cover design: Dolphin Associates
Printed in the UK

Published by R.A. Associates

*Dedicated to those who seek to imprison
the free spirit of humanity through the manipulation
and oppression of word and deed.*

You will never win.

*With love to our spiritual family
and all who have believed in us.*

*Readers should be aware that White Feather's teachings
are exclusively oral and the contents of this book have
been transcribed from live recordings of his communications
between 1998 - 2001. Wherever possible the text remains
true to the spoken word and only the punctuation has been
added in the interests of continuity.*

Contents

Introduction

The words contained within this third book of spiritual teachings are taken from recordings of 'Trance Evenings' held throughout the United Kingdom over the last few years. We have had the pleasure of serving many churches and addressing many souls and of giving them the opportunity of hearing the guide 'White Feather' speaking directly to them through the mediumship of Robert Goodwin. This has given a chance to gain a valuable insight into life in the spirit world and a deeper understanding of life's complex issues.

The hope is that, with greater spiritual awareness we can all apply this knowledge in our everyday lives. When at times there seems to be few explanations to the troubles of the world, the upliftment he imparts is most welcome to those who listen.

The evenings take the form of an introductory talk on trance mediumship and the use of these states in spirit communication. After an address by the guide for about twenty minutes, a question and answer session lasting about an hour, follows. We have found that it is important to show the audience the difference between Robert and White Feather. Although the guide uses the medium's vocal chords and some words from his unconscious mind there is a distinct difference in the voice. The rhetorical nature of the words used is also obvious. Having had numerous opportunities to get

I

get to know both gentlemen I can say that their personalities *are* different and although it has been suggested by some that they are one and the same, it is clear to me that they could not be. When all is said and done it is the message, not the messenger that really matters.

Robert would be the first to say that he could not possibly speak in the eloquent and learned way of White Feather and it is also true that even being privy to this wonderful philosophy on a regular basis we both, at times have our own battles in applying it personally! We realise that we are not perfect. We would not be on the earth plane if we were. This incarnation is another learning experience and with that wisdom and knowledge comes the responsibility to modify our thoughts and actions. It is not always easy for any of us to do this but our desire to learn and evolve spiritually helps in our quest to polish another 'facet of the diamond'.

It may sound to those who have not had the experience of seeing a trance medium that these meetings are a terribly serious affair - nothing could be further from the truth! White Feather's very dry sense of humour has had many an audience laughing. This is wonderful to be part of and the energies of the room are lifted greatly which is very often why he says something funny. He can also be very sensitive to those he speaks to. There have been occasions, (I think particularly of an incident in Tamworth when he spoke to a lady with cancer) when you could have heard a pin drop. There were many a tearful eye at his response to her question. He has the ability to have the answer as soon as the question has ended. There is no prior knowledge of the questions and although the subject may be specific he will still broaden the answer to include philosophy to help all those present.

Having chaired many times I have found it is best to wait until he feels he can answer no more. I have been caught out previously when I thought he had finished and intuitively he has known there is someone with an important question that needs his attention and I have been directed accordingly.

I feel very privileged to have been able to get to know more about the guide's nature and although he very rarely speaks about himself the loving, sensitive and deeply respectful qualities he has have come through many times and it is a most humbling experience. No subject is out of bounds, no creed, colour or religious persuasion is an obstacle and on many occasions the controversial subjects are those he delights in addressing! I have witnessed his responses to those who have little knowledge and those who have a great deal and his humility is ever present to both. We know that there are others in spirit who stand at his side during these intercessions and it is interesting to note that if the guide needs to, he will refer to his colleagues in the spirit world. It is also known that there is discussion and debate on spiritual issues among our spirit friends in their world and deliberation on subsequent subject matters which may be beneficial to impart.

Topical issues such as 'Foot and Mouth' and the awful events of the recent terrorist attacks on America have been tackled, helping us to see the bigger picture, the wider spiritual implications of governmental decisions and human responses that attempt to herd us into thinking as a collective, uniform group rather than to utilise our need and desire to think and speak as individuals. It is refreshing to be reminded that we can say no and reject the 'party line' if we feel deeply that something is not right. Using our intuition and trusting in the guiding light of our higher self we *can* make different choices than our personality might and our imprisoned minds may with understanding and knowledge, come to know the infinite possibilities of a life without boundaries. Appreciating that we are on this plane for such a short time with a limited view and that our decisions, actions and thoughts have long reaching effects on our soul's energy that can know no death. As we hold the thought that we all have a personal responsibility for the seeds we plant, nurture and harvest, we must endeavour to take that responsibility seriously and hold it in all humility and reverence so that in our own small way we can be an effective part in the effort to change the whole. If we seek the truth, adhere to spiritual laws and develop our armoury of love, understanding and tolerance we then, as a whole can make a significant difference in the mad, illusionary world that we live in.

We hope that in giving our time to link with those in spirit we can refine those positive vibrations, helping to find a pathway from ignorance to knowledge and give those who feel they have no choice, new opportunities to open their hearts and minds to the all encompassing spiritual love that is available to everyone if we could only allow that attunement to be realised.

We truly hope that you find something of value in the following pages and if these words only touch the heart of one soul that is a wonderful achievement.

We give our thanks and love to our spirit helpers and hope that they will continue to enable us to impart their teachings for a long time to come.

Amanda Terrado
February 2002

Answers for an Enquiring Mind

"You ask me from whence cometh my inspiration?
Is it not from those who themselves are inspired?"

Chapter 1
Guiding Lights

The very topic of spirit guides is one which fascinates all who are witnesses to demonstrations given through mediums worldwide and the debate as to whether a person has actually received the communication directly from a discarnate mind or, as is sometimes believed by those who doubt the authenticity of spirit intervention, from the individual's own unconscious mind is one which is still open to debate. Here, White Feather, who has demonstrated on numerous occasions that he is indeed a separate entity from his medium, answers questions put to him by those seeking to expand their understanding on the subject:

Q: *"How can someone who is developing as a medium, know whether it is a spirit person talking to them or whether it is their own thinking?"*

White Feather: " It is a question of discrimination and experience. You know when you first begin to develop and allow the qualities of your higher self to unfold through mediumship, there very often is accompanying this development, self doubt. Where one disbelieves and questions whether one is actually, truthfully upon the right pathway. Whether it is a figment of the imagination, or whether or not it is truly from spirit. This is perfectly natural, whenever you commence any form of development, whether it is learning to read, write, or even taking your first step, you stumble, you fall, you make mistakes and yet you persist, you carry on, you continue and it is the same with mediumship. You will find that if you learn to trust those in my world who work with you, that energy will get stronger and that tiny whisper will grow into a loud booming voice that cannot be doubted because you will hear it clearly and when that occurs you will know absolutely that you are upon the right path. Do not doubt the power of the spirit that seeks to operate through you because it is as powerful an energy as you will ever find in existence. It has guided you thus far and it will continue to do so. Does that help you?"

Questioner: "Yes it does thank you."

Q: "Do you only work through Robert or do you work through others and do we have different guides as we develop?"

White Feather: "Let me tell you that it is difficult enough working through this instrument without having to take up others! **[There was much laughter from the audience in response to White Feather's answer]**
In answer to your question, the degree of intimacy that is required to enable a link such as this to operate to the satisfaction which I require takes a great deal of effort and training. Not only from my world but also on behalf of the medium and it is a fact that where this degree of control is obtained it is not easily repeatable with other instruments. I know of no guide in my world who works through more than one medium at the same time.
You may very often find that you hear the same name but often this reflects not an individual but a group of individuals, a collective if you like, in my world who share the same conscious pool of knowledge and who operate through one or more mediums. But as individuals - no. We develop with that medium and in my case I linked with this instrument before he came into the physical body and I will continue to operate through him as long as I am able to do so, and I will not then operate through another. Do you understand that? It was a very good question."

Q: "I heard some philosophy a few weeks ago saying that our guides are only parts of our higher self, not separate entities. What do you feel about this? Also, why do some people develop quickly and others sit for years and still do not develop as mediums?"

White Feather: "Well you know it makes me question whether I really exist! **[Laughter]** But you know of course there is that aspect of yourself which one

2

can term a higher guide, the spirit guide, because you have your own higher knowledge that is a part of your soul and that, very often you know, when conditions are right, will help you and will guide you. But let me say quite categorically that there are many in my world, myself included, who are quite separate entities, individuals, humans like you, quite separate from our mediums and instruments.

Often you know, it is a source of great frustration to me when I seek to link with this instrument as I know it is for many other of my compatriots, for we have to cope with the various idiosyncrasies of the mind of the medium, of the health of the medium, of the thoughts and emotions of the medium and these present many barriers to us. So I wish that it could be easier, but let me say to you that I am indeed distinct from this individual and I always will be even though we are linked through the same motivating factor of wishing to serve the Great Spirit through love. Does that help you?"

Although pleased with the answer, the questioner persisted with the second part of her original question, concerning the development of mediumship only to draw this eloquent and metaphorical reply from the spirit sage:

Questioner: *"Yes.....but why do some people take a lifetime to develop?"*

White Feather: " Because it is when the fruit is ripe that it falls from the tree. If you seek to pick it before it is ripe, then it is very difficult to tempt it from the branches. When it is ready you have only to hold out your hand and touch it and it falls into your palm. It is the same with individuals who have come into this physical body at this time, because they have a service to render which mediumship plays a part in. There are others who are not yet ready here in this lifetime to offer that service and yet they think that they are and they often expend a great energy trying to develop to no avail because they are not yet ready. It is not upon their pathway, and whilst one can sympathise and have a certain amount of empathy and compassion towards their efforts it is nevertheless not their moment, not their time and we have to direct our efforts to those whose time it is. Whose time it is upon this world to operate as the form of a medium to enable this power to be made manifest to humanity."

Q: *"What kind of work do you do to reach the highest level and how do you progress?*

White Feather: " Working through this instrument and speaking to souls such as you, to you all, is my way of helping myself because you know, in giving service then one also receives. There is no loss without gain. There is no giving without receiving and service is the passport of the soul. It is through service that one develops and unfolds and each of you, however insignificant you may think yourselves, however small, however minute.....however you think of yourselves and see yourselves......you are all part of the Great Spirit and you can all render service and through giving service you will be served and you will evolve. That is how the law operates. I take no greater joy than this; speaking to you and allowing this great knowledge of the spirit to be made available to you."

On another occasion, when discussing the subject of spirit guides a lady in the audience wished to know whether we have more than one spirit guide working with us. In his reply White Feather once again emphasises the need for a spirit guide to establish a close link with their medium in order for the work to be successful:

White Feather: "There are several spirit guides who work with you. Depending upon the individual and the nature of their earthly journey there can be many, many guides and helpers who are drawn into a group that works, particularly where mediumistic qualities are evident. Where there is a spiritual undertaking to be performed, there you will find that there are many guides that link. There may be but one or two that actually utilise the gifts of the person, or the instrument, but others will also add their contribution. If I can say to you that I am the only spokesman, by and large, who works through this medium because of the intimate nature of the work involved and the close affinity needed to work at this level.

But there are many who stand at my side to whom I refer and who operate in other capacities through, and with this instrument. So it depends upon the work to be undertaken. Those who are not involved in mediumistic work, who are here perhaps to learn particular lessons, are nevertheless accompanied by one or more helpers who will try to......not interfere, because that is not possible with their freewill.....but try to influence and guide them in a purposeful spiritual way along the pathway. Does that help you?"

Questioner: "Yes, thank you very much."

Following on from the spirit teacher's answer, another of those present wished to know more about how those resident in the spirit world 'guided' us along our pathway and if they were able to help us with particular problems if we asked them:

White Feather: "Always there is guidance. You may not always want the answer that we give you, in the way that we give it. It is not always, as has been demonstrated I believe, quite adequately in some respects to you tonight......it is not quite as simple as asking a question and gaining an answer. But I can say that where there is an honest desire to learn and to receive help to a problem, whether it is mental, physical, spiritual or emotional, then we will do our best to give it.

When the lamb cries out, always it is heard, and never are you brushed aside or overlooked or forgotten. Where there is a genuine cry for help then there is someone who will hear it and who is drawn to you, without any doubt.

The problem of course, is two fold. Firstly we cannot always communicate directly with you, we have to come through a third party, through a medium and secondly, have you earned the right spiritually, to have the answer and to find the solution? Let me say this to you......and if I can draw on one who is so often referred to as 'The Son of God', but who was in my view a great medium, a great teacher......because you are all the Sons of God.....the Nazarene gave healing to many souls upon your world and yet he could touch one, and heal one and not the other. There have been many, many such healers and mediums throughout your history and you will find that where one is healed, the same power cannot touch the other. One foot that is crippled may be straightened, the other is left untouched. Why? Because that individual has not earned the right. You hear very often of the wonderful 'miracles' as they are termed, of the Nazarene, which are nothing more than the operation of cause and effect through natural law and mediumship. 'Miracles' don't occur, but you hear of them, you read of them but you do not hear of the failures. You do not hear of those who could not be touched, who could not be healed.

So you have to understand that there is a vast network of law that operates here and you have to try to look not through the eyes of matter but with the eyes of the spirit."

Q: *"Thank you. In addition to that, do spirits have a language barrier problem when communicating with each other and when they receive a message from someone whose native tongue is not English?"*

White Feather: "Essentially, no. Because we communicate through the power of thought and the language problem is not a barrier, and when we communicate with your world we communicate with thought. But where we have to perform in a particular way we utilise an instrument such as the one I am utilising now and speak through that instrument to such as yourselves.

There has to be a degree of education and I in particular had to learn and master the language and the words of your English language in order to speak through this instrument, even though I still employ the thought processes you understand, because here we are dealing on a different level than mere spirits from mind to mind. We are dealing through the physical level and we have to use the language that you understand. So we have to employ the thought processes and the language that is there within the medium's mind.

In my world we do not have the same difficulty. We can communicate through the power of thought and language is not the same barrier as it is here."

As is so often the case when White Feather begins answering questions put to him by a large gathering, his frequently detailed replies bring about a broadening of the themes under discussion and leads to many individuals being prompted to ask questions which they might otherwise not have considered. This is perhaps the true beauty of philosophical debate and the guide has himself commented on numerous occasions just how much he enjoys the stimulus of discussing the innumerable topics which are raised by those of an enquiring mind. Here, whilst still on the subject of spirit guides, a gentleman enquires about the nature of time and how it affects those in the spirit world, particularly when called upon to link with our world:

Q: " *Time is very important and we are governed by it on this plane* **[Earth]**. *Do you in the spirit world have the same difficulties and is there a feeling that in some way you too are governed by it? Is there, in fact any passage of time in the spirit world?*"

White Feather: "Well I have to say to you that there is, even though I listen with some incredulity sometimes to those in your world who think they know so much about my world who say that there is no time in the spirit world. How often have you heard that?! There is no time in the spirit world?

There IS time, but there is a different perception of it than in your world. But nevertheless we are aware of the passage of time. If we were not - at the level at which I am now - if we were not, then we would have no sense of past and no awareness of future. So we ARE aware of the passage of time. I know that a certain amount of time has elapsed since I began linking with this instrument. I know that a certain amount of time has elapsed tonight and I sense that from the level at which I am **[the spirit world]** even though I am working closely with your level **[the Earth]**. So we are aware of the

6

passage of time, but it is different, I have to say, than in your world, and the higher one evolves into the spirit world, the way time is perceived also changes.

We are able to see, for example, a little further ahead in time from a great vantage point in the higher realms of spirit than you can down here in the valley of the material world. Time is different. Time is also different in your world, did you know that? How often have you been standing, waiting for something? Perhaps in a queue, and a few moments seems like an hour, or many hours? And then, you can be enjoying something, some pastime or hobby and time seems to fly by. So what is time? It is a perception. Even though there is a movement, there is a flow, it is the way that you perceive it that is perhaps of the greatest importance."

Q: "You have answered my next question in some way, but is there anything else you would like to say to someone wanting to know how spirit people actually progress? Do they move to a higher plane in the spirit world? Do they move from one place .....do they go over to another? Could you explain more about that?

It appeared, by the nature of the question that the gentleman was enquiring whether or not spirit guides, and indeed all of those resident in the spirit world remained in one place or evolved to other levels. This is what the spirit sage had to say about spiritual progression:

" All of life is a procession. It is a progress from the lower to the higher, from darkness to light, from ignorance to truth, from captivity to freedom. And that begins from the moment you came into being, whenever that was, as an individualised spirit soul, and it continues through the various planes of my world. Always there is this desire to progress. There is this desire to move into a refined state of thought and of being. Even those in the lower realms of my world who are trapped there temporarily by their own thoughts, their own superstitions and ignorance, even in them the divine spark is not extinguished and even though they are not aware of it there is still the same desire to progress and to learn and to unfold. And I say to you this; that perfection is never reached, even though it is the heart's desire, it is never reached. If it were, then life would become a monotony. It would be boredom. You would learn no more, you would not move. You would find that life would become stagnant and stale. There has to be this constant striving and that is as it should be because that is the very essence of life itself. Ultimately it will become the greatest expression of the Great Spirit that you can be."

Q: *"Can spirits come back from the higher planes?"*

White Feather: "Only to a point. If you were able to be elevated to the top of the tallest mountain in your world and then asked to communicate to someone in the valley, in the deepest valley, you could not do it because there would be such a vast gulf, distance between you. So you would either have to come down the mountainside or the recipient would have to climb up from the valley and somewhere in between the two extremes you would perhaps meet. But in my world, where there are those who have reached a certain level of spiritual evolution, they cannot return to that point because it is impossible for them to do so. So they have to come back through an intermediate state - they have to come through a medium.

There are mediums in my world as there are in your world and sometimes what you hear when it is of the highest teaching, comes not merely from the communicator who works with the medium but from a higher source. It is like a waterfall. It is a reciprocal effect. As I speak to you I am also linking with higher minds in my world and if there is a question which I cannot answer, then it comes to me from those that know more than I do and this is as it should be. So always try to understand that there is this link and where you reach a certain point, you cannot return to the lower because the lesser cannot contain the greater.

Let me say one more thing to you, which you might find interesting; I operate through the astral body of a Red Man. Were I to move beyond your earth plane, beyond the astral.....if I were able to grow spiritually and return to the highest level that I could achieve and decide not to link ever again with this medium or this earth plane of yours.....that astral body through which I come would disintegrate because there would be no further purpose for it. The fact that I have chosen to return enables me to keep that astral body in its state so that I can use it when I draw close to your earth. Do you understand that? And it is useful for me to work through that body because I know it. It was a body that I once had in it's physical equivalent upon the earth, so I know it, and I have been able to keep it for this purpose. This may sound very deep to you when perhaps it is very new and you cannot fully understand it, but this is why we have to link through the astral body when we link with a medium upon the earth plane.

Where there is a length of time that has elapsed in the progression that has taken place, the gulf between the higher and the lower is so vast that it cannot be bridged - there is no point of contact. Perhaps if I can put it a more crude way; if I said to you 'can you speak to the frog that sits in the pond at the bottom of the garden and tell him of the laws of physics' you could not. You could have a good go, but I doubt if he would understand you. But if you were able to communicate through another frog, a similar message, then perhaps you would have a chance. So you understand the difficulties we have. We have to employ your language. We have to deal with your prejudice, with your fears, with your superstitions. We have to surmount so many barriers and obstacles in order to convey even a small essence of the totality of the truth.

It is very difficult. It is at times frustrating. But always it is rewarding, because if we can help but one of you then we have achieved a great deal."

Q: "I have been told that we all have spirit guides such as yourself who come to people like me. But tell me, if people are grumpy and bad tempered and if as you say 'like attracts like', then does it mean that you will not get a guide that is calming and even tempered?"

White Feather: "It is not quite as simple as that! I can't quite paint the same black and white picture that you do or that has been painted for you. You all have those who stand by your side. You do not all have spirit guides as such because what I consider to be a guide is one who seeks to operate through mediumship to bring teachings and messages, help and healing and guidance to humanity. But you all have helpers. None of you are ever alone. You have those who are drawn to you out of an affinity of mind and spirit, so they have the same character, they are in essence as you. Nevertheless they are drawn to you because they have a greater understanding also. If they do not have that understanding, if they are not equipped to work with you in that way because they have not learned the lessons, then they are not ready. They are not permitted to become a helper, or as you call them, a guide.

So you must remember that those who do work with you are of a deeper understanding. They have a little more knowledge and understanding and spiritual unfoldment than you do. That is why they work with you and always try to give you the benefit of that benevolence and that wisdom, that understanding, and impinge upon your mind and upon your spirit whenever they can to help you and guide you and uplift you.

So if you are grumpy, that is a matter for you. We cannot stop you being grumpy! What we can do is help you to try to uplift yourselves beyond the emotions to the higher energies of the spirit where you will embrace a greater truth and a greater power than I can put into words."

Q: "Do you have a name and what do you see when you work through this medium?"

White Feather: "It depends upon which level I am operating. The name which I could give you if you wish is of little consequence because it is the teachings which I impart, rather than the personality, which I seek to convey to you. The name you can refer to me is White Feather. I have nothing more to say about myself other than I have lived upon your world and manifested many times upon your world through different cultures and races.

As to what I see depends upon what level I am operating and which attributes of the instrument through whom I work, I choose to employ. If you are referring to what I can see at the moment......I cannot see your physical bodies. I can see aspects of your etheric bodies which appear to me as regions of light. If you are referring to what I see in my world.....I see many things of great beauty through my eyes as you see through your eyes. I also see through my mind, as you do, because you interpret what you see within your mind.

In my world there are wondrous places, vast expanses of land, fields, oceans, mountainsides. We have great cities, we have places of worship, we have great libraries and temples and the most wonderful architecture, the most beautiful scenery that is so rich and verdant in its colour and even colours that do not express themselves upon your world. So it depends upon which level I operate and which level to which you refer, but I hope that has helped you in some way. Thank you."

Q: "Are spirits particular over the quality of a person who works for them? Could someone who has been bad in life still become a medium?"

White Feather: "Are spirit particular over the quality? Well, let me say that we have to operate through a mind with whom we have an affinity, with whom we can work and operate through. If there is no point of contact then we cannot work through them, so we are not drawn to them. We are drawn to minds of a like nature, who are sensitive, who have a desire to serve as we do, to help humanity and to serve the Great Spirit. And where we find such instruments then we can be drawn to them and we ARE drawn to them naturally, through a natural process of attraction. And we can operate through them in accordance with our ability to develop their potential and bring the wondrous bounty of the spirit into manifestation upon your earth. Is that to what you were referring?"

Q: "Yes, but what about if a person wants to become a medium?"

White Feather: "Well, there are many aspects to be considered. Firstly, you cannot suddenly decide to become a medium. You are either mediumistic or you are not. You can attempt to develop those qualities that you may or may not have inherent within you and if you have them then they will develop when the time is right. But it is not a question of one suddenly deciding to become a medium.

As to the manner in which you have lived your life, it is not a question of being able to wipe the slate clean, neither is it a question of anyone standing in judgement over you, because we are all imperfect, myself included, and we have a great deal yet to learn and to unfold. But the very nature of the way that you live your life determines the sensitivity that is there or is not there. If you have lived a life, shall we say of selfishness, where you thought only of yourself, where perhaps you have inflicted suffering or pain upon another, then you cannot suddenly expect to be able to blossom as a medium and draw those minds from my world who would operate through you because there would be no point of contact. If however, you have lived a life where you have tried your best to serve, where you have always tried to help others and you have the gift of mediumship, then you will find that those minds in my world will be drawn to you. It is a simple question of who you truly are. And let me add this also: you know there are many in your world who are painted as being bad, whatever that means,because they do not fit a certain criteria, a certain way of thinking or acting and others say they are bad when in truth they are nothing of the kind. They are in fact good, but because they do not fit the status quo they are rejected out of hand. They are pushed aside, they are trampled upon, they are pushed down. But we see through that veil. We see through that mask. We see the real person. That is what matters to me.

When I look at you I am not interested whether you are a man or a woman, whether you are a child, whether you are black or white, yellow or red. It does not bother me. What concerns me is what is in your heart, what is in your spirit and I seek to look within the person. Not at the mask but within the self. That is what matters."

Q: "Can our helpers change as we develop spiritually?"

White Feather: "If it is appropriate yes, you will find that it is so. Because one mind, one individual can take you so far and no further. Then it is that another may choose to link with you out of the group, to take you a little step further. And perhaps another again, may take you further still. In my personal experience I have linked with this instrument since before he chose to reincarnate into this physical body and I will continue to work through him as long as I am able to under the circumstances."

11

On another occasion whilst discussing spirit guides the wise teacher pointed out that spirit guides such as he would have themselves undergone experiences that had brought about a 'similar' state of spiritual evolution, once again underlining the law that 'like attracts like'.

Q: "Would my spirit guide have gone through some of the same circumstances as I have gone through?"

White Feather: "Not necessarily, but they will have arrived at a similar state of spiritual evolution to that of yours, but a little more advanced. Do you understand? It is not always so that they have undertaken the precise experiences that you have, because if I may coin a phrase which I often employ, 'there are many paths that lead to one place'. The fact is, they are drawn to you because they are of a similar vibration. That is what is important. They would not be drawn to you if they had no understanding whatsoever, or no empathy with your circumstances, even though they themselves may learn from you. The fact is that if they are classed as guides or helpers, to work through you they must have that empathy. They must have that understanding of your circumstances, otherwise they would not be drawn to you."

Q: "When we work with a guide or helper, is it possible then, that we progress together?"

White Feather: "Yes, there is always progress. As I have already said, I learn from touching you in your world. I learn from you as I hope you learn from me also and so progress is made on all levels. I would never be so closed minded or arrogant to say to you that I cannot learn anything else, that I cannot learn from you, because that is not so. One can learn from everything and every experience. I often say you know, when I am giving my talks to those in your world; 'look at the fool - he will teach you much. Listen to that which is silent - it will speak to you. Look at that which is still - you will find movement within it. Look not always at the great evolved soul. Look at the simpleton, look at those who work in the field. Look at those all around you, who perhaps you consider to be lesser than you. You will find that in some way they are greater than you.' So you can learn from everyone and everything and certainly progress is made not only in your world but by us in ours."

Q: *"Can you tell us how many planes of attainment there are in the spirit world and what level you are on?"*

White Feather: " I haven't counted them all yet and I don't know of anyone that has! **[Laughter]** You know I always have a chuckle to myself when I hear it said by some 'illumined mind' that there are seven levels or nine levels or ten levels, or whatever, because I don't know how they have counted them all! The truth is, that the levels in my world correspond to the minds and the souls that express themselves upon them, and because life is eternal, because life is infinite, there is an infinite expression and a progression for every soul and every collective. So you might find perhaps that this is a concept new to you. But let me say to you that there are levels yet in my world which have still to be unfolded, which have yet to be formed because there is not the mind, there are not the individuals who are there to exist upon that level. Do you see? The level is created if you like, by the thought processes, by the character, by the spirit, by the soul that inhabits it. It is then, the same the other way, to the lower levels of darkness and ignorance for even there, there are levels of 'evil', if you want to use that word, of darkness and ignorance, of depravity, which it perpetuates through its own actions. This is opposed to the levels of light which are there for the soul which seeks to advance itself.

With regard to the level at which I exist, it would be the third level from your world. If you count your world as level four, for simplicities sake, the first level beyond that being the 'summerland', or the 'astral plane' as it is referred to, then I am two above that."

Often, at gatherings where the spirit world communication involves either deep trance or physical mediumship, the energies employed can be greatly affected by the thoughts and emotions of those present. This is why, the spirit helpers and guides will often interject a note of humour into the proceedings in order to 'raise' the vibrations and thus help the communication to flow more easily. White Feather is a master of this, and in answering the next member of the audience his mischevious sense of humour is all too evident:

Q: *"Did you choose to come back to enlighten us? What was your profession when you were here? Were you more advanced than many and what were your choices in coming back?"*

White Feather: "You know, she is very clever how she asks several questions in one! I must learn to perfect that art! You know, as to my profession, I had no profession as you would recognise it. As to whether I chose to come back, of course there is always choice. You are not compelled, I was not compelled to return to link with your world and those of you who choose to re-enter the body of matter will not be compelled to do so. It is always a matter of choice which is allied to spiritual unfoldment and understanding. In my case, I chose to return to strive to deliver a knowledge, which I felt I could do and which would assist those in your world and humanity in general in reaching the level of spiritual understanding, which is indeed the goal of everyone in your world.

At times I find it difficult, frustrating, hard, because linking with your world and all of the things which obtain here upon the earth plane requires sacrifice. Indeed, I am compelled to sacrifice progress in my world. But I do it out of choice. I do so gladly, that in giving service I too can receive from you and that through this exchange, humanity, myself and those in my world can benefit. So it is an exchange of information and a service that I render gladly.

Are you all enjoying yourselves? You know humour is a very serious business! You have to lighten up you know, because you are surrounded by so much love. You are surrounded by so much light. I look into your hearts and I see that you are fearful, some of you. You worry too much. Never worry. Do not be fearful. You are of the spirit. You are indestructible. Be happy."

Not everyone appreciates the work which the spirit work undertakes in order to allow guides such as White Feather to operate through their chosen medium. A great deal of time, effort, dedication and discipline is necessary on all sides in order for the necessary close links to be forged. Often, the guide will comment on the difficulties involved in producing good trance mediumship and there is a notable difference to be observed between what is referred to as 'psuedo trance' and 'real trance' mediumship.

True trance mediumship requires an extremely close bond between guide and medium. Often, this is so close as to be undetectable, with only very subtle changes in voice tone, phraseology and grammar being observed. This, opposed to the sometimes blatant posturing and 'pigeon English' put forward by less credible exponents.

Those witnessing a White Feather demonstration, will undoubtedly notice the former changes occurring, with a definite voice shift and a clearly distinguishable alteration in the language patterns, tonality and general phrasing of the speech. However, there are still those who find it hard to accept that a separate entity from another world is

communicating with them. Whether this is because of the pre-conditioning that is inflicted upon so many in this world or because of a lack of education and awareness of spiritual and psychic matters is open to question. What cannot be denied however, is the quality of White Feather's oratory and his undoubted knowledge and wisdom. Never has he been known to fail to answer a question and always, his response is immediate and without a moments pause for thought, a true trademark of genuine trance mediumship.

Here, in true fashion, he deals with a question put to him by a well known medium during a public demonstration:

Q: *"I am not keen on the descriptive use of the words 'Trance Mediumship' because all forms of mediumship involve and altered state of consciousness. What level of an altered state of consciousness would you class actually as trance mediumship?"*

White Feather: "I do also concur with what you have said. There is very little understanding of the altered state in your world because there are many states which can be regarded as altered states. As to whether one is crossing the threshold as it were, where one enters into what is termed and recognised by some in your world as a trance state, is one which is widely misunderstood. If I were to simplify matters for you, I would say that the state of trance can be determined by the point at which contact is made by one in my world to work sufficiently through one in your world and to bring a greater expression of mind energy and spirit controlled teachings and knowledge and wisdom and whatever service is being rendered, through that instrument. As to the exact point of reference where that is reached, it is difficult to express it in your earthly language. But you will know instinctively within yourself.

I know son, that you are developing and enabling this aspect of your mediumship to come to the fore. Is that not so?"

Questioner: *"Yes."*

White Feather: "Then you will find that the state that you are seeking will gradually, gradually increase and deepen as your development takes place. You know, I've heard it said, quite wrongly.....even by those who are considered enlightened in your world......that there are several levels of trance....there are nine levels of trance......there are twelve levels of trance.....I don't know who measured them, but I regard trance as like a river that flows and the deeper that one goes, the greater the expression of the spirit that can manifest through you. Do not think that you will wake up tomorrow or the day after and you will have developed the trance state. It will be a gradual, natural process, a deepening process where there will be more of the spirit and less of you. And that is as it should be. Does that help you at all?"

Questioner: "Yes......yes."

White Feather: "But you have more........?"

Questioner: "Yes. What bothers me is that I'm aware of people influencing me and I am conscious of what they want to say.....and sometimes I think that the words should come without me having to think about them or being aware of them before they are said......and that bothers me. How much is the words of me and how much of the words is of them **[Spirit]** *?"*

White Feather: "And how much does it bother you when you work with your clairvoyance?"

Questioner: "Nowhere near as much."

White Feather: " Because you do not think about it, that's why. You go with it, and you must do the same son, with this work. If we were able......if we were able to erase your conscious, rational thinking, if we were able to close your mind and just put the power of the spirit through it, then it would be very easy. We cannot do that. The mind is a living entity, we have to work with it. You will never find, that even with the deepest trance states.....and I say to you quite categorically son......that even with the deepest trance states you will find there is still an aspect of your consciousness that is present within the teachings. Only within the very deepest states attainable is the mind of the medium almost, but not totally, pushed to one side. The advice that I would give to you is to 'go with the flow' of information that is coming with you. Do not think about it greatly. Just allow it to flow through you as you do when you are engaged in your other work and you will find in this way....and I have to tell you from those who work with you.....you will find that in this way your trance state will deepen quite quickly. More than you anticipate at present."

Questioner:" Thank you for that help."

White Feather **[turning to another medium seated close by]** "Do you have a question also?"

Medium: "I do yes."

White Feather: "How did I know that?"

Medium: "As a medium who works in trance I'm often aware of peoples scepticism and doubts when viewing trance, however good the quality. What are the benefits, other than direct communication, of working in trance in this way for people?"

White Feather: "Because in a true state of trance it is more of spirit and less of the medium. I have always said through this medium that the true expression of trance should be judged not necessarily by the information given but by the way that it is given. By the truth, naturally, that is contained within it, but by the manner that it is given, in that it flows. Where you have individuals who, perhaps for ulterior motives like to elaborate in some way.....where you have unnecessary posturing, changes of voice and mannerisms which are totally uncharacteristic and do not reflect the mind that seeks to work through them, then you are right to cast doubt upon the validity of it. True trance mediumship is a blending of minds, where the medium's mind can be overridden to the point where the greater expression of the spirit energy can manifest through it. And this, you will find, is characterised in many ways; firstly, you have not heard me hesitate tonight in answering a question because I know what is in your hearts and I know that I have the answer there for you. Is that not so? And you will find that also I have worked in a way that is in accordance with the level of under-standing. I have not patronised you. I have not talked down to you. I have indeed enabled the expression of the spirit to work through this instrument in a manner that is befitting the spirit, and it is this that characterises trance. Not by one who says 'I am this person......I am that soul....I am this......I have been that.....I am the other.....that does not account for a great deal which is why I do not elaborate upon my identity and personality. It is only a name that you can have for reference. What matters is the truth that comes through and the way that it flows through. That is what characterises good trance. It is for you to decide ultimately, but that is the criteria upon which I would base my decision. Does that help you?"

Medium: "Why then do you feel there is the need for the spirit world to communicate through trance? Because I have had this conversation many times with my own helpers and friends in spirit?"

White Feather: "I can only refer to the point I made earlier in that the greater the control that can be obtained, the more of the spirit and the less colouration of the mind of the medium there is present. You must recognise, as your brother has already stated quite correctly, that all mediumship is in essence an altered state. Trance is an altered state. The object of mediumship, in its utmost, in its most refined and wonderful state, is to remove the medium's mind and consciousness to the point where the expression of the spirit can be all but purified through it and the 'trance state' as you refer to it, or the altered state, enables that to be obtained in much greater degree than simply 'overshadowing'. Do you understand that?
I am speaking now from my own viewpoint on this side of life. Where we have an instrument who is, for whatever reason, consciously or unconsciously obstructing the power of the spirit through the colouration of his own thoughts and desires and wishes......and very often this IS unconscious I must add.....then it prevents us from allowing the purity of the spirit power to manifest. The deeper we can take the instrument, the more of the power of the spirit, the less of the mind of the medium is apparent. That is why we employ this faculty of mediumship. Does that help you?"

Medium: "Hmmmm............"

White Feather: "Are you sure?"

Medium: "No."

White Feather: ".....because you know, you must always be truthful with me. Because I will know if you are not."

Medium: "The point I am trying to make is......I know from my own point of view the need for it, but what of those who watch?"

White Feather: " Well of course, they must, as I have already said use their reasoning, critical faculty and if you want to believe that I am a figment of someone's imagination then you are quite at liberty to do so! But if you do, then please consider what I have said to you in the form of the truth which I have delivered because it is that which is of the greatest import. That is what matters.
In all form of mediumship you must use your reasoning faculty and if you wish to disregard it then do so. You won't offend me. You may......you are at

liberty to disregard it. That is what you must choose. But if you decide that there is some aspect of truth and reality within it, then take it within you and enable it to enrich you and bring you into a deeper understanding because that is the purpose of all mediumship. Now does that help you?"

Medium: "It does."

White Feather: "Good. Thank you for that."

On a somewhat lighter note, came a question from a deep thinking gentleman with a wry sense of humour concerning the origins of spirit guides and the way in which some mediums envisage their helpers from the next world:

Q: "In spiritualist circles there does appear to be a preponderance of spirit guides who claim to originate in the Americas, Tibet, China and Egypt. Why is it that there is a real shortage of East End of London bricklayers and Glaswegian welders? Could this be due to the human desire to associate spirituality with ancient aesthetic practice? For example, it is difficult for many to conceive that the man known to us as the Nazarene could possibly be married and the father of children as has been suggested by some. Your comments please."

White Feather: "I absolutely concur with what you say. There is very often a desire, individually and collectively to be associated with a guide or a helper or a teacher who belongs to a particular tradition that is regarded as being spiritual. You know, we have to be content with this. Sometimes a medium or developing instrument will have an idea at a subconscious level that their helper, their guide, their teacher is of a particular persuasion. That he is an Indian or a Chinese or a Red Man or anything that they care to dwell upon and when that individual, that spirit teacher in my world links with them and begins to work with them, the developing medium projects that. As in the case of angels, they project that. They believe that is what they are going to see. They believe that is the mind and the teacher that will be drawn to them and so they project that, and we have to contend with that. We have to work with it. Sometimes it is easier for us to go along with it to a degree because there are more important issues at hand, one of which is bringing the truth through that individual. So we have to contend with it and when the time is right then we can reveal ourselves, when that medium has developed sufficiently to see us truly. We can step forward and reveal ourselves as we truly are. Let me say that there are many teachers and many

19

guides in my world that lived very ordinary, one would say mundane lives upon your earth. There have been numerous instances I could give you of names who have worked through well known mediums and who have revealed themselves as being Irish or Cockney or even those who are of the black races upon your earth and who are not regarded in the same way as the Tibetan or the Red Man or the Chinaman and that is sad because they are just as evolved. They are just as worthy and just as great in their service of the Great Spirit. But it is not always that they fit what is expected. They do not fit the imagination of the medium. This is what we have to contend with. Do you understand that?"

Questioner: "Yes I do, thank you."

"If you scowl at the lion, he will turn upon you.
Yet if you sing to him, he will lie at your feet."

Chapter 2
Kindred Spirits

The animal kingdom is an aspect of creation very close to White Feather's heart and he often speaks with deep respect and great affection of the contribution which animals make to our lives. He also shares the great sorrow which many of us feel in the way that the animal kingdom is treated by man, particularly the exploitation and lack of respect shown to many species by those whose ignorance of the spiritual dimension of nature is all too apparent.

In the United Kingdom, where most of White Feather's teachings are recorded, a devastating outbreak of foot and mouth disease, leading to the slaughter of literally millions of animals, often brought about deep and searching questions asked of the guide by those whose lives had been affected by the mass cull. Here, along with other enquiries concerning animals and the afterlife, are a few of those questions, put to him by some of the many caring souls who attended the spirit sage's talks during this difficult period. But firstly, the messenger from beyond begins with an address to all of those present:

White Feather: "Good evening. May I greet you all with the divine light and the radiant love of the Great Spirit. It is always a great honour and privilege to have this opportunity to speak with you and I pay my usual tribute to the infallible operation of natural spirit law that ensures that the veil which often separates our two worlds can once again be lifted to enable this bridgehead to be forged across which I can help assist the great benign power of the spirit to flow into your hearts and minds. And although this is something which I have undertaken on many occasions in the past it is something with which I am always pleased to be a participant.

For your world is filled with ignorance, but where there are those lighthouses of the spirit who radiate from within the desire to enable the divine essence to radiate and shine through them, there it is that many lost and weary souls can find solace and guidance and comfort.

There are a great many myths and misconceptions you know, spoken about my world and those of its inhabitants, but let let me say as I often do to dispel some of these misconceptions, that we are like you, human in every regard. We are not angels with harps, we are human beings who have a body that is as solid and as permanent as it can be and as real as yours. I see through eyes, I hear through ears and I speak through my mouth. I have limbs just as you do. I am human in every regard, with weaknesses and strengths just as you. The only difference between us is that the vibration upon which I operate is of a finer, swifter vibration than your world which is very gross and slow.....sluggish compared to the spirit world.

Like you I have a great deal yet to unfold and develop. I have many lessons to learn, many truths to discover. But if I can this night share a few of those which I have been fortunate enough to have imbibed, then I will be satisfied. There are many questions I know, that arc in your minds and I will give you the opportunity in a little while to ask them, but I thought I would say a few brief words to you tonight concerning the great difficulty and suffering that is apparent all around you in your part of the earth at the moment, particularly with the animal kingdom. And I have to say quite categorically that the resulting suffering that is taking place within aspects of the animal kingdom is as a direct result of man's inhumanity in the systems that he employs which are often brought about and guided by financial impetus and reward. Man must understand that what he does to his fellow man, what he does to the beast of the field, what he does to nature he also does to himself and even though disease and suffering are a part of the physical domain, nevertheless that suffering has been enhanced and multiplied by the neglect and ignorance that man shows for his fellow creature upon the earth. Man you know, thinks that he is the master of the creature of the field. He thinks he is the master of nature and he shows a great arrogance and disrespect for the operation of its laws, but everything has its consequences and what man does to others he does to himself because the law of cause and effect operates with a ceaseless perfection and must outwork itself. Man cannot blindly neglect the feelings of the animal kingdom, the suffering that they feel, in the pursuit of profit. And where this ignorance persists then you will find, as you have already, that there are all manner of diseases and pestilence and suffering that is inflicted firstly upon the animal kingdom and then ultimately through the food chain to humanity.

Do not mistake what I am saying. You know, it is not each and every one of you that is a participant in this, but you will find that it affects humanity as a whole and is a result of man's ignorance. It also raises of course, further questions in regard to the suffering of the animal kingdom and the reasons behind it. Very often you know, I am asked the question 'why does the Great Spirit, why does God permit suffering to innocent creatures?' You must understand that wherever there is suffering, there is a reason behind it. There are lessons to be learned and always there is compensation and retribution to follow.

The animal kingdom is somewhat different in regard to its spiritual progression, spiritual journey, than that of humanity and to understand this more fully you will perhaps have to understand the very nature of yourself. You are parts of God. God is not separate from you. You are each part of the Great Spirit and you come into form, you come through form of a physical nature in order to gain experience, in order to gain expression and to allow the divine within you to unfold itself and to express itself. You, my friends, have come through the animal kingdom. You have come through the bird and the fish and the beast of the field. Not you the individual, but you as part of the Great Spirit. Now the animals to which we are referring for the purposes of this talk tonight are part of a group soul, part of a group consciousness, and through the suffering that is being undertaken by them upon the earth, that group consciousness is progressing. It is being compensated and ultimately there will be those aspects that, having come through that level of being will come into a higher form of being such as the human, and when that is reached, there the soul has individual status.

You, having come through those lower forms will never return to that level. Even though you may come back time and time again upon the earth through different human forms you will not go back into that group consciousness because you have attained an individual status and it is for you to continue on your upward journey through your world and through mine, ever progressing. But that raises in itself a very important point; that you have a responsibility. Because the more that you unfold, the more that you are spiritually aware, the greater the responsibility that you have. Not only to yourselves but to those of a lesser order, of a lesser awareness than you. You cannot simply ride roughshod over them and expect them to be subservient to your every will and whim and desire. Humility of a true state is where the evolved soul can bend down and bow down in gratitude before the humble flower or beast of the field and know that it is one and the same. Where you have those who are elevated to the status of the 'great I am' and placed upon pedestals and worshipped, there you have a soul in decline. There you have a soul who is about to stumble and fall through its own self importance, brought about by ignorance. A truly evolved soul is humble and recognises its part in the great scheme of life of which it is a part of everything that is.

You and I, although we are the same, we are different. Although we are different we are the same. Although we are parts of individuals, we are parts of one whole. You are not any greater than the lowest insect in your world and there is no one in my world, however evolved they are, that is greater than you. This you must understand.

Now, you may say to me, what of the consequences of the suffering that is continuing to be perpetuated around you.....well, it will not alleviate, it will not go away. In fact it will return periodically until man learns to change his attitude towards life, until he changes his methods. And this will only come through education, through understanding, through spiritual awareness and unfoldment and each of you, although you may think that spiritually, you are impotent......that you can do nothing to change the ways of the world.....you can, because each of you moves within your own orbit and you can each influence, not through pressure or oppression or through force, but in a quiet way, those whom come into your orbit by speaking of the truth as you know it and understand it.

As I have said many times; if you want to change the whole you have to change its constituent parts and if you can help but one soul and they in turn help another, then you will find that like a ripple spreading out from the centre, many are touched. And eventually the balance begins to tip and ultimately perhaps there will become a greater awareness of your world than there is now. It is something to think upon. Perhaps you can, when you can see the suffering of the creatures of the fields, send your thoughts to them. Not only to the humans that are in contact but to the creatures themselves. For in doing so you will help the soul consciousness of that group to progress."

Q: "How many animals return to the sprit world?"

White Feather: "You have to understand the nature of spirit life and its operation with your world. All of life is spirit. There is no life without spirit, there is no spirit without life. So in the essence of the answer I give to you, ALL life returns to spirit. In truth, it is never separated from spirit. Those creatures who do not have the advantage, if I can refer to it in that way, of communication with human life......which enables their soul to forward itself and advance itself because of the personal contact...... those who do not enjoy that opportunity return to what I refer to as the group soul of that species. Where you have those creatures in your world who enjoy a close affinity with humanity that often encompasses love and companionship, what you would refer to perhaps as 'pets' - a word which I do not care for, but which you will understand - then the soul is furthered, it is advanced. Then, upon the point of death that individual creature maintains its individuality for as long as it is necessary and appropriate for it do so in my world. Do you understand that? Does it help you?"

Questioner: "Yes it does. Thank you very much indeed."

In answering the next question, the spirit guide once again underlined that where there is suffering, there is also compensation, but also emphasised the price which mankind will have to pay for acts of cruelty towards animals:

Q: "I am very concerned about the animal kingdom, especially those slaughtered for meat. I am very aware of their suffering. What do you in the spirit world think about this?"

White Feather: "I must say that we are also aware of their suffering and I say that even though the one through whom I speak does consume meat. But you must recognise that there is compensation for the suffering in that the soul of that species is helped and compensated. It is not always compensated in a physical sense upon your world, but there is compensation nevertheless for all the suffering that is undertaken by creatures and indeed humans upon your world. I only wish and pray and hope that we can sufficiently educate humanity into the full realisation that he is indeed with his animal brethren. That the spirit that now operates through humanity has in its time come through the animal kingdom and indeed, what he now does to his world he does also to himself.

So what is sown must be reaped. Man is not here to have dominion over the animal kingdom, to persecute them and utilise them for his own wealth or his own material ends. He must be aware they are here to help him, to live alongside him. They have untold benefits and wealth that he has yet to recognise. When that realisation finally comes it will be a great day, in my view."

Q: *"When people are vegetarian, are they more spiritually evolved? Does a meat-eater take upon themselves the suffering of the animal?"*

White Feather: "I know some very ignorant vegetarians and I know some very intelligent and evolved meat eaters, so it does not always follow. I know the point you are trying to make and where there is a spiritual, a true spiritual awareness and responsibility, and the conscience that comes with it, there you will find that, that soul does not partake of the eating of meat. I wish that it were so with many in your world but it is not for me to pass judgement upon those who eat meat and those who do not. But as a rule it follows that with the evolution of the soul, the individual no longer partakes of the flesh of the beasts of your world because they realise that often the suffering and the pain that has gone into the destruction of their body to feed the human in that way is against natural law."

Q: *"But what about the creature's suffering...is it becoming a part of them?"*

White Feather: "Who?"

Q: *"The person who eats the meat*

White Feather: "Not necessarily, not necessarily. But if you are referring to the fear that the beast feels before it is destroyed then that fear.....yes it goes into the creatures flesh, not only physically in the chemicals that are released into the blood, and the toxins, but the mental aspect is also there within the etheric that is around the meat that is eaten. So in that respect yes it is - you are quite right in stating that. "

On another occasion a member of the audience raised the subject of 'pet euthanasia' challenging White Feather's earlier comments that it is wrong to take life, whatever the circumstances. The question brought about an interesting exchange of opinions and an uncompromising and perhaps controversial response from the guide:

Q: *"Sometimes we have to take our pets to the vets to have them put down and end their suffering. Isn't that euthanasia?"*

White Feather: "It is, and the same principle applies, and I can't change it I'm afraid. I know again that the compassion which is part of the soul quality is a very good motive and I would be the last one to judge you or anyone for acting through that compassion, but I have to say that there is still a limited understanding of spiritual realities because your world is always geared towards physical life, that you have to keep the physical body alive and prevent suffering at all costs. Now whilst I know that it is a very admirable trait and it is a very admirable thing for any healer to try and prevent suffering, I have to say that with the greater spiritual vision it is not the be all and end all. Because the greatest lessons in life are very often learned through suffering and by taking away the physical body, however great the motive, it is not always the answer.

It's a difficult one I know, and one which will perhaps tug you this way and that, but I can only say that in the passing of time and with the greater understanding you will perhaps see things a little differently than you do here in the midst of it."

Questioner: "May I just come back on that question. If we kept an animal in dire pain we would be in trouble with the RSPCA. What then? How could you stand it yourself if an animal or human was in such pain? It puts us in a dilemma."

White Feather: "But you see, you are trying to....if I may say....judge eternal principles by man-made laws. If I say to you 'if you are trying to claim a piece of land for yourself then you will upset a great many people who will say that it is not your land, it is our land' then you would have to face the consequences of it, but in true spiritual terms it is not their land, you would have as much right to walk upon it as they do. So the problem here you see, is that we are applying spiritual laws and spiritual principles in the framework of man-made principles and man-made laws and it is those man-made laws that you here upon the earth have to adhere to and live by. That is why I understand the difficulties that arise. But that does not alter by one iota the greater spiritual laws that are the reality of life. You have to see the difficulty here. I understand what you are saying but you are applying that to man-made laws when you talk about the RSPCA and the results of your actions. That is a man-made institution."

Questioner: "Could you then, let an animal live on in pain?"

White Feather: "Well again, that would be a question for my own conscience and I would make a decision based upon the level of awareness that I had reached at that time. But I can say now quite clearly to you that I see things differently from the spiritual side of life than I would have done upon the earth and did do upon the earth."

Questioner: "Well, you are only upon the third plane. You already told us that."

White Feather: "Well, I have a great deal to learn......as do we all."

Whilst the gentleman concerned did not appear to accept the views of the spirit sage, the main 'bone of contention' seemed to be whether or not it is 'spiritual' to allow suffering to continue or whether it is the act of a more 'evolved' soul to put an end to that suffering. When pondering upon this subject we should perhaps pause to reflect that if we choose to end that pain through love and compassion we will not be judged or condemned for it. It is after all, the motive which counts above all else and we ourselves are measured as much by that as by the act itself. The point that White Feather appears often to make is that suffering, be it of animal or man, is an experience which the soul draws to itself in order to grow and to evolve towards a higher awareness. As he frequently states 'suffering is the shell that encloses understanding' and even though it seems spiritually right to attempt to alleviate all pain, at what point do we actually deny the soul its opportunity of learning a greater lesson through that suffering and is the taking of life, even through the motive of compassion a denial of the outworking of spiritual law? It is for you, the reader to decide what to believe, but without question the debate on euthanasia will long continue.

Finally, a question which was asked during a trance demonstration in Aberaeron (an area with neighbouring farming communities) during the height of a serious Foot and Mouth epidemic which hit the United Kingdom and some parts of Europe during 2001. The guide's response, whilst challenging and thought provoking also brought tears to the eyes of many of those present as his words reached out with love and compassion to the animal kingdom:

Q: "Could you comment on the current outbreak of foot and mouth disease in the British Isles. Are we dealing with spiritual lessons that are to be learned from this situation and are we dealing with it in the best possible way?"

White Feather: "There are lessons to be learned from many, many different situations and scenarios. I do not believe that the people in charge of operations governing the outbreak are dealing with it in the right way because at the higher echelons of government there are ulterior motives at work. And let me say......and this may surprise some of you......that there are ulterior motives and hidden agendas that you have little or no understanding or awareness of. It has brought about, and continues to bring about a manipulation of circumstances for political ends, for political purposes.

Humanity should be aware that this is unfolding, because it will have dire consequences, not only in the short term but in the longer term for the freedom of humanity. It is a great shame and indeed fills many in my world, including myself, with deep sorrow that animals that are innocent in the respect that they are the victims of this which is being perpetrated, have to undergo such pain and suffering. The group soul that comes through these creatures, please let me say to you, compensates for the suffering. The losers in this are humanity. Because what man does to his fellow creatures he does to himself.

Let me say something to you. It is not for me to tell you how to pray. Not for me to tell you what to think or what to do, but perhaps in your quietest moments you can send out a thought for all those innocent creatures in their suffering. The thought that you send out will reach them and will help the soul express itself through them. They cannot speak to us in words. They cannot say, "Help me", as a child can or as a victim of some other act, in a human sense. A creature of the field cannot speak and it helps when you send thoughts to it. If these thoughts are of the right motive then they are never wasted and I can assure you, from this side of life, that when you send thoughts to these creatures, it helps them in their passing and the group soul to progress. Perhaps you would do that."

" All men walk upon the path of light,
but some walk backwards and see only life's shadows. "

Chapter 3
Troubled Minds

White Feather is often asked questions relating to suicide and those who encounter difficulties and suffering both upon the earth and in the next world. Here he offers hope and comfort to some of those whose lives have been touched by the pain of troubled minds:

Q: "What happens to the spirit of those who have committed suicide?"

White Feather: "It depends upon the level of their awareness and understanding. There is no judgement from those in my world or by the Great Spirit. The individual judges themselves, but you have to realise that there are different reasons, different motives which have to be taken into consideration when discussing suicide. There are those who take their physical body, who destroy their physical body because their mind is in turmoil and because their thought processes are not rational. There is an imbalance there. There are others who have taken their own lives because they wish to hurt others, those who destroy themselves by violent means because they wish to harm others......and their motive is different. So the motive is what counts and the greater the knowledge, the greater the responsibility, and there is a price to be paid for every act that is undertaken. Where there is greater knowledge the price to be paid is far greater than where there is ignorance. You have personal experience of this?"

Questioner: "Yes I do."

White Feather: "I thought so. Then what I would say to you is; do not judge, send your thoughts to the one who has undertaken this act and you will find that they will be helped by your love and compassion and understanding. And that will be reflected back to you, do you understand that?"

Questioner: "Yes, thank you."

Amanda [Chair] "As a follow on to that question, there is a written question here from a member of the audience [Although White Feather prefers verbal questions, some people are often too shy to ask and so are given the opportunity to write down their question instead] What happens when we first go over to the other side and is it true that when that happens there are always loved ones there to help us?"

White Feather: "You are never in a situation, when you pass into my world, when the physical body drops away, when the silver cord severs at the moment of death.......you are never in a position where you are alone. You are always met by someone. Very often it is through a link of love that you are greeted and always there are loving hands to help you make that transition from the lower to the higher. No one is ever discarded or over-looked, or neglected or forgotten. As to what awaits you, that is dependent upon you as an individual. Upon how you have lived your life. Upon the Karma that you have created. Upon that which you have sown - which must always be reaped in direct proportion to that which has been sown. The law always works with a mathematical precision, remember that. And you will find yourself, in normal circumstances, gravitating to the plane which best befits your soul and the progress, or lack of it, that has been made."

Q: "Will our guides or just our loved ones be there to greet us when we pass?"

White Feather: "Well, I like to think that if you have guides they are loved ones also, because where there is a desire with one to link through another - that is one in my world to link with you - there has to be a love, otherwise there would be no attraction in the first place. But you will be met by those with whom you have the strongest link of love. whether that is your helper, guide, family or friends it does not matter which. As long as the link of love is there you will be met because no one, NO ONE passes into my world alone. That is a fact. No one. Do you understand that? Thank you for the question."

Returning to the theme of suicide, another member of the audience wanted to know if those who take their own lives are welcomed in the spirit world. In his gentle, but firm manner the wise teacher from beyond once again reassured all of those present that there is no judgement:

Q: "Are suicides welcomed in your world?"

White Feather: "Absolutely, we do not judge individuals like you do. We do not judge in the same way. Always you know, where there is a suicide, there is a reason for it. Sometimes the individual takes their own life because their mind has been touched and because they are in a state of confusion and so they take their own life. But we do not judge them as you do.
Often they are met by loved ones, they are met by love and they are surrounded by love and they are welcomed into my world and helped to realise what they have done. Very often their actions are undertaken when their mind is disturbed and there is ignorance and confusion. We do not judge, we accept them for what they are, we point out to them why they have done what they have done and we try to help them. Do you understand that?"

Questioner: "Yes, but what about those who, because of their actions go to a lower level in your world? Are they also helped?"

White Feather: "Absolutely. Sometimes you know, those who take their own life go onto a lower level in my world but they do not remain there. They place themselves there because that is the state of mind when they commit that act, but ultimately they come out of that darkness and they return to the light because that is where they are meant to be. And where there is love there is no separation."

Another of those present had also submitted a written question concerning those souls who 'do not make a smooth transition' to the next life. Her concern was that they might in someway be 'lost' or 'in limbo'. Whilst reiterating that sometimes there can be a temporary difficulty due to the state of their mind at passing White Feather was

particularly careful to emphasise that the soul of the individual is not harmed by this transitionary phase of its passing:

White Feather: "........the reason that some individuals, upon making the transition from your world into the world of spirit, become 'lost', to use your terminology, although no one is truly lost......is because of their state of mind. And very often where there is a sudden passing, perhaps a violent one or one caused by what you would refer to as an accident, or perhaps where there has been a lot of suffering of the physical body through a lengthy illness, then this has had a temporary effect upon the thought processes and upon the mind. Then it can be that upon the point of death the individual concerned is in a place that is not truly befitting the place that they should be at. Equally, you can find that someone has a particular belief system, perhaps a strong religious belief or even a belief that the spirit world is non-existent, an atheistic belief, and this also will affect to a degree what happens and what occurs when death takes place.

But I must stress that the soul itself is not harmed or touched by this. It is only a question of the personality and the strong thought and emotional element that is present at the moment of death. Do not think that anyone in my world is left in limbo or somehow gravitates to the lower planes or is lost in some way, because that does not occur.

There can be, as I have said a temporary delay because of the nature of the thought processes but always there is someone there to help and to guide and I know of no-one who has been 'lost', whatever that may mean. Ultimately we all find our way through natural law to the place where we are meant to be. We gravitate to that particular plane. I don't know if that helps you at all?"

Questioner (finding the courage to speak to the guide: "Thank you."

White Feather: "If it does not, you must say and we will speak at greater length......."

Questioner: "No, it does help me very much. Thank you."

Q: "What is your understanding of schizophrenia?"

White Feather: "Well, it is a matter of the physical apparatus not befitting the operation of the mind and the spirit through it. There are no schizophrenics in the spirit world. It is a matter of an imbalance, a malfunction if you like in the physical brain, in the physical form, that prevents the mind and the soul and the spirit from expressing through that physical form as it should do in the natural state of things. So again, you have to look at the whole and judge and reach your understanding from that spiritual viewpoint."

Q: "So when someone is tormented by evil spirits these are not then lower entities from the spirit world?"

White Feather: "I didn't say that. Because it may well be that. That is a different scenario. Where there are souls who, for whatever reason have opened themselves up to the lower levels of my world, they may be judged and viewed in your world as being schizophrenic when in reality they are not schizophrenic in the true sense of the word but through their actions, which you may or may not be aware of, they have in some way opened themselves up to those lower planes and the entities upon them. And there are indeed those of a lower nature in my world who take great joy in creating mischief, in drawing themselves, through the law of attraction to those minds whom they can torment. If they can gain through assisting those in your world to create mischief then it gives them great delight and it is a problem that we have to deal with. So you have to look again and assess whether that individual is truly schizophrenic or whether through some way and some means they have opened themselves up to the lower astral planes of my world. There may be a difference."

Q: "Could you tell me, when someone is in a coma for a long time what happens to the soul during that period?"

White Feather: "You must understand that the physical body has many imperfections and what the coma is, is not a spiritual imperfection or a mind imperfection. It is an imperfection of the way that the spirit and mind work through the body and work through the brain. And even though the physical body appears to be comatose , and is not always able to recognise and hear sounds, and is unaware of its environment, even if this is the case, the soul and the mind which expresses itself through it is at liberty to withdraw to a point and can experience things on another level. These are not always remembered. Just as you, when you have a dream and an experience in the sleep state don't always remember it. - you only have snatches of it when you awaken. But you are aware that something has happened on another level because your mind is not held by your body or by your brain.
A coma state is an inability of the mind and the spirit to function correctly through the brain and through the body. Do you understand that? You have to make that distinction."

Whilst suffering of all kinds may be difficult for us to understand and to deal with, it is perhaps the suffering of young children that affects many of us so deeply. When that suffering is perpetrated deliberately it becomes increasingly hard for us to rationalise how and why people are so cruel and what response we should undertake. The following question came from a lady directly involved with the prison parole services, whose dilemma became quite apparent when she asked the guide what actions society should take:

Q: *"My question is about the innocence of children. In one of your books you speak about the innocence of children, what we can learn from them. So many people grieve for small children who perpetrate acts of evil. Those boys who killed the young boy ......do we keep them locked away from the rest of us or do we allow them back into society?"*

White Feather: " That is quite an in-depth question. In actual fact, what I was referring to was a general scenario of the innocence of children. Of course there are exceptions to every rule. There are bad apples in every bunch and of course there are those who perpetrate acts against their fellow man of which age is no barrier. What you have to recognise is that there are some souls who reincarnate into matter, into a young body, but they are actually an old soul and they bring that badness with them. And they can perpetrate acts in a different form because that is what they have brought with them from a different life.

Again, there are exceptions to the rule, but as to the two individuals in question, again you have to have this balance in your world. Do you shut them away to protect the rest of society or do you educate them and let them free because they are so young? All these things you must weigh up and consider. All that I would say is that those who make the decisions do not always do so from the viewpoint of their higher self. They do it from their lower self. They do it to gain popularity, to gain votes or they do it for other purposes.

In an ideal society children in general, not just those who are locked away, would be taught spiritual values from a very early age. They would be taught in your schools not just about history, but about true spiritual realities and learning to be kind to life, to others. Learning to serve, learning to love, to have compassion, to have tolerance, to have understanding. You live in a society that is 'the society of want', the society of the self, that demands for itself and wants instant results. This will be the downfall of humanity.

So you see it is a very deep question and one which can be opened up into a whole raft of other issues which can be considered. Always I come back to the simple teachings of spiritual truth; that if you give unto others, if you do unto others that which you would have them do unto you, then you will not go far wrong. And that is a simple rule of thumb, but unfortunately that knowledge has all but been eradicated from your society. That is at the roots of where it is wrong. That is where the foundations upon which all else is built are crumbling. That is what has to be addressed."

Q: "Why is it that some people go through more pain and hurt than others?"

White Feather: "Because through the laws of cause and effect, and Karma......which is a very just law may I say......you create, you sow, you reap. You are where you are today because of what you were yesterday, because of what you thought and did and said, your motives. You will be where you are tomorrow or in a thousand years because of what you are today. So it is all a question of receiving that which, in reality you have created yourselves.

You know, when there are those who argue against reincarnation I always say this to them; why is it that in some lives on your earth there is so much pain and suffering whilst others seem to sail through untouched and seem to have everything at their fingertips, where life is a bed of roses. Where is the justice in that If it were not for the fact that there is balance in life and one has to return time and time again in order to experience all that is. You cannot do it in one lifetime. You have to know darkness to know light, you have to have been male to know female, female to know male. You have to have been ignorant to know truth. You have to experience this vast panorama of life with all its joys and sorrows, all its captivity and freedom, in order to come to a central place of balance.

Remember this when you are at your lowest ebb; that it is always darkest before the dawn and if the pendulum has swung one way now it will surely swing back the other very soon."

Q: "In this world there are so many emotions.......pain, greed, envy....what emotions are felt in your world?"

White Feather: "Any emotions that are felt in your world can also be felt in my world. We are not devoid of emotions. We are not emotionless robots and we are not perfect. There are many in your world who have great emotions in a positive or a negative way and just because they are removed from the body of matter at death and continue in my world it does not mean that they are necessarily divorced of these emotional states, particularly where they are very strong. So anything that is felt in your world can also be

37

experienced in an emotional way in my world because you still have an emotional body. All that I will say to you is that there is an opportunity in my world to overcome those emotional states. To learn perhaps, in a different way than you could encased in a body of matter. To understand the effects that they have upon the mind and upon the spirit, and through progress, through moving into the higher realms of my world one gains mastery over one's emotions and one gains mastery over oneself. And that is a great thing. It is perhaps the greatest thing of all - to know oneself and to have control over oneself."

In answering a lady who had inquired of the spirit master whether people who had passed 'tragically' by such means as drowning, and who had suffered greatly prior to death actually remembered their traumatic experiences in the spirit realm, the guide gave an insight into how the spirit helpers assisted such troubled minds to adjust to their new life. He began by placing emphasis once more on the depth of unfoldment which every individual has acquired:

White Feather: ".........it depends upon the level of spiritual knowledge and awareness they had prior to passing, but let me say that very often you know, what appears to be great suffering to the physical body is not so to the spirit and to the mind. Very often when I have witnessed passings into my world the physical body appears to be in the throes of turmoil and pain and suffering, yet the spirit has already begun to depart and there is not the same level of consciousness and awareness, so the suffering is not felt by the individual. You must understand that.

As to whether they remember, then that is another matter altogether. Sometimes there is a recollection, at other times there is not. But let me say to you this; there are many in your world who do indeed pass in very difficult circumstances but we have in my world what I would call the 'Halls of Forgetfulness' where one can be taken and it is is rather like washing over the mind with a loving energy that erases those experiences that were so traumatic, so difficult, that they would continue to cause distress to the soul. The learning, the knowledge, the understanding is kept intact, but the horror, the heartache, the despair, the pain, is removed and the soul is healed. It is balanced again. So do not worry, do not concern yourself. Do not grieve that your beloved is still in the midst of suffering by remembering the trauma of the experience because I can assure you that is not so. I hope that is of some help?"

Questioner: "Yes, but how long does it take for the suffering to be erased?"

White Feather: "It depends upon the nature of the suffering. If, for example an individual has through his own freewill undertaken to cause suffering to others and them himself or herself passes in such circumstances that are very traumatic, then a law has been set into operation and what has been sown must be reaped.

When I speak of the 'Halls of Forgetfulness', I speak of those who, shall I say, are 'innocent' of the cause of their passing, even though you must understand that accidents do not occur because all is regulated by law. But where one has earned the right to have that suffering and the memory of that trauma removed, then it can be removed very quickly. If one has not earned the right, perhaps because one has been an individual who has inflicted suffering upon another, then the memory and the pain associated with that passing will remain and will indeed cause further suffering until that individual is ready to move forward.

It is not a question of being condemned to eternal suffering, or 'hell' or 'damnation', whatever they may be, it is a consequence of the operation of natural law. When one has earned the right, then one automatically receives redemption and compensation. When one has not earned the right then one has to wait and perhaps undergo further difficulties until such time that the balance can be redressed."

With so many troubled minds both here on earth and upon some levels of the spirit world we may be forgiven for thinking that we are impotent to help. But it is encouraging to know that there are many ways in which each of us can assist those in difficulty to be healed:

Q: "Is it possible that we as humans, with human emotions, feelings and thoughts are able to help the suffering in the world at this time?"

White Feather: "Absolutely, without question. Nothing is ever lost or wasted. You must remember that you operate within an ocean of energies, many of which are the result of the thoughts and actions of individuals and collectives. No thought is ever lost or wasted. No action is ever lost or wasted, particularly if its motive is to serve. There are so many ways that you can help in the world. Not only by helping those who come into your own orbit, either in a practical way or simply by listening to them or by speaking to them, offering them a kind thought or a kind deed, but also those who you consider to be many miles from you, perhaps in the midst of turmoil or war or destruction. You can help them by sending the power of your thought. Whether you choose to call that prayer or positive thinking, or whatever label you put upon it, it does not interest me. The point is that thoughts are real. They have a potency. They have an energy that is as real as you are and whenever you send thoughts in kindness and love, in altruism to help others, then those thoughts are registered within the atmosphere of your world and they will also reach those to whom they are sent. Whether or not those individuals are aware of it does not matter. The point is, all thought reaches its intended target.

So always be mindful of the fact that even though at times you may think that you are helpless, that you can do nothing to change events in the world, you indeed can. As I have said many times, 'The one will become the many and the many will become the one."

"Man has knowledge, but not wisdom.
He has intellect, but not understanding.
He has power, but not strength."

Chapter 4
Hidden Agenda

Whilst this is a book about universal truth and spiritual guidance, the discerning reader and thinker will appreciate the reasons surrounding the inclusion of this controversial chapter concerning the many changes now taking place upon the earth. Changes which will ultimately affect each and every one of us.

Whilst conspiracy theorists, political analysts and writers from all areas of life have put forward theories as to what appears to be unfolding around us, suggestive of a hidden world agenda perpetrated by a select 'few', often termed 'The Illuminati', the spirit world seems to have remained largely silent about these issues.

It cannot have escaped the notice of the reader that more and more restrictions are being placed upon humanity which are ushering in a world of control and manipulation. At first covert, and now more and more commonplace, mankind is becoming enslaved by the systems which have been put in place by businesses and governments world-wide to control his very being. How long will it be before there is a world army, a world bank, a world government and a micro-chipped population enslaved and controlled by the few who appear to have the power over the many?

Whilst White Feather and his spirit world contemporaries seldom elaborate upon the affairs of mankind, preferring instead to focus upon universal truths which extend far beyond the boundaries of our world, more and more there appears to be a growing concern in the spirit world as to the future of humanity. After all, what man does to himself and the earth affects directly future generations of souls who may wish to reincarnate.

Perhaps the time is fast approaching for all of us to question whether or not we are prepared to allow the global manipulation of our thinking, our actions and our very way of life to be altered to suit the agenda of those whose motives are anything but spiritual, or whether we are willing to fight for what we know to our divine heritage; the truth that we are individualised, reasoning, spiritual beings.

Here are a selection of comments made by White Feather and drawn from recordings made at various gatherings over the last few years:

Q: "I was giving healing recently and I saw clairvoyantly the changes to come......people were frightened.......I was told that we should not be getting clairvoyance when we give healing but all the same we don't yet know the evil to come. Is this true?"

White Feather: "Well let me say there is a great darkness which is yet to emerge upon the earth and I don't wish to frighten or disturb any of you. But there are minds of the lower order which, even as I speak seek to manipulate thinking, to direct humanity into ways of manipulation and control that would deny the divine heritage of the spirit, which is the rightful heritage of all of you. You have to be vigilant and aware of any form of control of your thinking and actions, anything that erodes your freewill and freedom of thought.

You often think that you live in a democracy but you do not, because even as I speak to you, you are controlled and manipulated in ways of which you are not always aware. So you have to learn to be wary of the propaganda that is given to you and to use your reasoning mind. Because certainly what you are fed through your media, through your newspapers and your television bears little resemblance to the reality of things and the example which you gave in the way in which healing is sought to be controlled and manipulated is only the tip of the iceberg.

There needs to be, as I have often said, a revolution. Not a violent, bloody revolution, but a revolution of thought and of action where you as individuals can take power back to yourselves, not be controlled and hand it over to governments and companies who manipulate and whose desire is wealth and material possessions. That is not right. The real power in your world lies within you as individuals and when humanity collectively begins to realise that, then and only then will there be any radical changes. But I am afraid that there will be a darkness which will come upon the earth before there is light. But do not despair because there is a plan which is unfolding. These things are known and even though man can hinder and delay and even destroy to a point, he cannot prevent the outworking of the plan because always remember this; the universe and everything contained within it has been devised and continues to exist through perfect mind. The mind of the Great Spirit. Always remember that matter is servant, spirit is master."

Speaking about the same subject on another occasion, the guide answered a question about the world's 'changing energies' and hinted that these were in fact spiritual energies which were attempting to 'quicken' humanities vibrations in order to counterbalance the lower vibrational energies which were engulfing the world at this time:

Q: *"You have said previously that there would be some major changes in the world. Recently there has been some 'unrest' in our supply of energy and people have not responded as anticipated. Is this the start of those changes that you referred to?"*

White Feather: "As I have already said there is an undercurrent......whether I would use the word awareness I don't know.....but an undercurrent within humanity, an inkling at some level that things are not right. That things are not as they should be. There is a restlessness.....man's spirit is restless because he knows that there are those who have another agenda and who seek to manipulate and control his spirit and the spirit will never be subdued and controlled and forced into channels where it is never intended to go. So there is this restlessness and there are many in your world who sense this, who feel this vibration but don't understand it. They don't know why they are restless, they just know that things aren't as they should be. This is because of the energies that are now coming into your world that are encouraging this and this will grow. You will find that it will grow and get stronger."

The spirit sage went on to explain that there would be difficult times ahead for the world as those forces seeking to control civilisation intensified their efforts whilst higher energies from the spirit planes sought to counterbalance the negative effects by bringing about an increased awareness and sensitivity within mankind:

" I have to say that there will be clashes, there will be unrest, there will be times when the forces of negativity and positivity meet head on and there will be all kinds of upset. But you know, there has to be change in order for a new way of thinking to be born and very often it is from the ashes that the phoenix rises. What you are seeing are the first instances, the first flourishes if you like, the first skirmishes of that which is to follow.

Do not misunderstand, I never advocate violence in any form, but there has to be a challenging directive, there has to be a revolution.....not a revolution that is a bloody revolution, but a revolution of thinking, and very often this involves tearing down the old before the new can come through."

Continuing his theme, White Feather drew upon an analogy with nature and explained how decay inevitably gives way to new growth:

"You know, many, many centuries ago when I was upon your earth we learned how to respect nature and we learned how the elements would very often sweep something of great beauty away, to leave a place desolate. Then we would watch as the new shoots began to form and new life came to replace the old. And this is how the old order of thinking in your world, which is stagnating, is beginning to crumble.

You only have to look at religion and look at your orthodox churches, which are more empty than full because people are beginning to question, they will no longer accept the age old dogma and doctrine that has been spoon fed to them. They don't want it and it will be the same in all arenas, all areas of life. Politics, of which I do not speak very often, will be a prime area for change because the old systems of politics and the old way of doing things must give way to a greater and more spiritual, charitable way of living.

So what you are seeing are the first instances of this change, but it won't happen in your lifetime here on this earth at this time."

Perhaps one of the most dramatic events to affect humanity on a global scale came with the 'terrorist' attacks on America on September 11th 2001 which led to further restrictions of personal freedom and a demand for a 'war on terrorism'. After the enormous outpouring of grief caused by the outrages and the sorrow felt by millions worldwide came the cry for more identity cards, electronic surveillance and a further curtailing of personal freedom throughout the 'democratic' world in order for us to be 'protected' against further terrorist attacks. Whilst terrorism that advocates the use of violence to promote it's cause can never be justified, the more cynical amongst us have speculated that those who were the instigators of the attacks might

have been the very persons who appear to be now to be ushering in a 'New World Order' in which our basic liberty is called into question. Indeed, a well known historian and researcher has labelled this scenario 'PRS' or 'Problem-Reaction Solution', where a 'problem' is artificially manufactured, leading to an outcry of 'something must be done!' at which point a 'solution' is conveniently put forward by those whose agenda it was in the first instance.

A few days after the attacks on the Pentagon and the World Trade buildings in America, White Feather spoke to a gathering in Derby, England. His talk was both hard-hitting and sympathetic, but as always, contained the wisdom of a soul whose loyalties lie only with the truth:

White Feather: " ....your earth is a dark place, particularly at the moment. Where so many souls struggle under the weight of fear, oppression, superstition and ignorance. And it is the work of those of us who are engaged in linking with humanity to try to put into perspective the events which are unfolding and also to offer some comfort and enlightenment to those minds who are in need of it.

As I have said on many occasions, it is with great joy that we link in this way and I must emphasise as I link through this instrument that neither he nor I have any prior knowledge of any questions which we may later invite you to ask. And that is as it should be because true spirit communication is a spontaneous act. It is a linking of spirit, through spirit, to spirit. And real mediumship provides not only evidence of our world that lies beyond your earth but also offers humanity the guiding light of truth that will, if you imbibe it and take it within your very heart and being, provide a beacon to guide you along life's dark pathway.

Now there are many aspects of spiritual teaching and law upon which I could have chosen to speak to you tonight, but in view of the events which have transpired recently in your world I thought you might wish me to say a few words upon the matter. Because there is without doubt a great fear amongst many in your world. Fear is the enemy of the spirit. Fear is the enemy of all that is of truth and light, because fear saps, fear drains, fear vanquishes reason, fear prevents the higher energies of the spirit from expressing themselves as they should do. And yet your world is gripped at this time, by fear, because of the acts of some misguided individuals and groups in your world who think that they can sow seeds of destruction to bring about a harvest of peace. This can never be. Neither in my view, is it right that the response should be more aggression and destruction of life. Because an 'eye for an eye' as it is referred to in one of your books, is not the answer to advancing the spiritual progression and unfoldment of humanity. Man must learn, and this is where the difficulties arise, that he cannot apply earthly standards and earthly solutions as he sees them, to what is a more deeply profound spiritual problem. What do I mean by that? The problem is that man is ignorant, by and large, except for a few individuals who have some knowledge and understanding of the realities of life. And this ignorance is perpetuated from generation to generation, and this has been continuing for centuries, for aeons of time upon your world.

There have been civilisations in the past that have arisen and given birth to illumined minds but for various reasons these have crumbled and decayed only to have been replaced by the orders of dogma and creed, ceremony and ritual and rigid thinking and thought patterns that are perpetuated from generation to generation.

Where in your schools are there taught the lessons of spiritual love, of altruism, of giving not to receive, but in selflessness? Where are taught the lessons of the unity of all life, of the oneness of all life? They are not. Your children and your children's children and generations going back far into time and indeed perhaps into the future, will be taught the same myths, the same misgivings and misunderstandings that have been rolled out in 'parrot like fashion' time and time again. And this is the root cause of the problems in your world.

It is not 'God' that causes wars. It is not 'God' that has created religion. It is humanity. And whilst it is right that man should have different views and differing opinions, because as I have said many times 'many pathways lead to one place', the difficulties arise when the beliefs become so entrenched that the mind becomes closed, and you cannot enter a closed mind. It is impossible. It is only when that mind begins to melt in its thinking and opens its heart and its whole being to the infinite possibilities that lie beyond the rigid structures of its doctrines that it can begin to move forward. And that can only come through education. That is why these evenings are so important. You may think 'how can I influence world events?', but you can. Because as I always say; to alter the whole you must change the sum total of its parts and each of you is a part of the whole. You are all parts of the one universal family that is the Great Spirit and is humanity. And if your thinking can change, and that of your brother, and those who come within your orbit, then perhaps eventually there can be a movement, a shift away from ignorance towards a higher plateau of spiritual truth and understanding. But it is a long and difficult and arduous battle. For the enemies that you face are all around you. Not least are those who seek to manipulate the thinking of humanity for political and state purposes, for the advancement of certain 'world order's' that they believe will enslave humanity and will give power to the few, whilst controlling and manipulating the many, and until this can be challenged and changed it will perpetuate. And you will find that violence will breed violence, darkness will breed darkness, ignorance will breed ignorance, hatred will breed hatred. You have to change it, you have to challenge it. And whilst it is all very well, and admirable for you to send forth your thoughts - because thoughts are potent energies and very often powerful - there has to come a time when you stand up and be counted. When you can challenge your leaders and your governments and say 'this is not right, we have to change it'. It does not require violence, it requires that you, in a non-violent way challenge the thinking and say 'it does not have to be this way'.

You are wondering at the moment what world events will unfold and whether there will be conflict on a global scale in your world. Let me say that from the vantage point at which I stand I do not see that there will be global conflict but there will be an escalation of violence. There will be an escalation of man attacking man, brother against brother and this time is a very difficult one for your world. But you know there is an opportunity here, for man stands at a crossroads, to change thinking and move in a more spiritual direction. But that will only come about if you as individuals realise the power that you have. I have said on more than one occasion that there will be a time when the 'one will become the many, and the many will become the one'. At the moment those who have enlightenment are like an oasis in the desert, they are few and far between. They are scattered. There is a lone voice here, there is a lone voice there. There is a collective here that speaks and there is another there that listens, but they are few and far between. And it is only when the scales are tipped and the balance changes that real change can come about.

This is why we need to bring this truth, this philosophy, this reality through to humanity of what he truly is. Your scientists will tell you that man is a collection of electrical impulses and molecules and atoms that just happened to come into a state where consciousness appeared and life began. That is the great lie that is perpetuated. The other great lies are so numerous.....too numerous to mention. You see them all around you, given to you by minds that are as misguided as those who speak to you. You have to look through that. You have to see through the veneer. You have to strip away and reveal what is at the heart. You have to look with the eyes of the spirit, not with the yes of matter and that is difficult because this is a plane of illusion upon which you dwell. You think that it is reality - it is not. It is anything but reality. The real reality lies within here **[pointing at chest]** It is within your heart and within your thinking and your minds and your spirit. Because it is that which builds the reality for you. Think about it. You are where you are today and humanity is at the state that it has reached because of the previous generations that have gone before it. And you are where you are today because of what you were yesterday through your thinking and your actions which have placed you here now. As to where you will be tomorrow or in a thousand years, that depends on what you do and think and say now as I speak to you. The choices are now. The decisions have to be made now, and it is you, each of you who are the architects of your own destiny, your own journey, but more so that of humanity.

You cannot bear the responsibility of other's actions, only your own. But the fact is, the more that you know the greater that responsibility comes to bear upon you. 'Ignorance is bliss', so they say. Knowledge and wisdom is a difficult pathway to tread because it brings responsibility and it is that you have to act upon that responsibility.

We know that you make mistakes, that you err, you stumble, you fall, but we ask only that you adhere to that knowledge which you know to be right. And in these times of misinformation and confusion, how do you know what is right? Who to follow? Who to believe? Well, let me say to you this; that truth comes from within yourself. If you listen to someone or look at something, question it and if you find that it strikes a chord within your heart and you know that it is right and you believe that, then go with it. But if you cannot accept it, and that goes as much for what I am saying to you as any other, then reject it. Put it like a book upon the shelf and let it gather dust. Perhaps there will be a time when you will return to it.

For the time that is approaching now, you have to learn if you can, to put aside your predujice, put aside your fears, your anxieties and maybe even your anger, and learn to reside in the still small place that is at the heart of your being, which is the temple of the spirit. There is a saying you know in your world, that 'if you can keep your head whilst all about you are losing theirs......' This is what you have to do. There will be many voices that will speak to you in anger over the next few weeks and months. Learn to listen, to decide for yourself, but listen to your inner voice, it is the voice of the spirit. It may speak to you in but a whisper, but it is louder than any other voice that will speak to you over the coming period of time and it will always guide you correctly. The decisions that you make and that humanity makes in the time to come will have a profound effect, not only upon your lives but also upon those of your children and your grandchildren. And who knows, there may be a time when YOU wish to return to incarnate upon this world and you are the architects of that future generation."

Having stirred the hearts and minds of those present, the spirit ambassador wasted no time in answering the concerned questions of

those whom his words had touched, beginning with one regarding the passing of the many souls who lost their lives in the destruction which took place in New York and Washington on 11th September 2001:

Q: *"The many souls whom we have just lost to spirit......how did you deal with them and did they incarnate knowing that this would happen?"*

White Feather: " Yes, I know that this is a bone of contention with many within your movement and indeed many thinkers upon your world. First of all let me say that no-one is ever lost. When there is a passing, be it of one individual or many thousands, it is known beforehand and those souls are met by their loved ones in my world who meet them when the time for their passing arrives. As to whether they were meant to be there, this brings into question the whole aspect of law and its operation because many in your world will say 'well, it was an accident that an event happened and they happened to be there and so they passed through that accident...or through that act, be it accidental or malicious......they passed in those circumstances and it was fate or bad luck that they were there'. Well let me say to you that in an ordered universe that is governed by natural law, there is no chance, there is no fate, there is no such thing as luck. All is governed by law and if those individuals pass at that moment, be it through what is termed 'accidental' means or malicious actions as happened recently in your world, then it is because their energies placed them there at that moment. If they were not meant to have been there then they would not have been there.

Their soul let me say, as opposed to their personality.......their soul knows in advance the course of its life and even though all of life is not preordained there are certain events that are known by the higher self, by the soul, before that individual enters into your world. And even though man can shorten his life, even though he can change the course of it there are some things which cannot be changed.

There is a time to be born, there is a time to die, in the physical sense, and man cannot lengthen his life. He can shorten it, and there are certain aspects of that life time which, even though humanity has freewill, are there and which the soul knows of before it incarnates. So perhaps you can understand that all who pass in such a tragic event are there, not because of some fluke or fate or chance or random event, but because at the soul level their energies placed them there."

Q: *" Some forty-four years ago, I was witness to three H-Bombs being used. Do you know if there will be the use of such weapons of mass destruction in the future?"*

White Feather: "Well let me say that man has developed an awesome capability for destruction and there will be use at some point in the future of such weapons. You know, I have been asked the question before, if I can open this out a little, as to whether your nuclear energy is a bad thing and it is not this knowledge of how to split the atom that is a bad thing, it is not the nuclear energy that is bad, it is man's use of it that is bad.

You can have a knife and you can eat a meal with it or you can cut yourself or someone else. It is not the knife which is bad, it is the use of it. Man has knowledge that he has acquired through his discoveries in science, but he does not have the spiritual wisdom to accompany it. So his mental development, his intellectual development has gone one way and his spiritual development has not kept pace with it. Do you understand that?

Let me say that in regards to the question of nuclear capability, man cannot unlearn what he knows. It takes a great deal of time and the passing of generations for knowledge to be forgotten and in the short term man cannot unlearn what he knows. At the moment he is like a child with a box of matches and the temptation to use them grows daily. I believe there will be a time, perhaps not in the immediate future, when he will strike the matches. As to what will transpire depends upon many factors but perhaps man has to learn that lesson before he can realise the consequences of his actions and the true reality of what he undertakes through his ignorance.

Sometimes you know, you have to put your hand in the fire and be burned to understand the nature of it. You have to know darkness to know light. You have to know pain to know joy. You have have to have been in ignorance to come into truth. That is the hard lesson and this is the plane of hard lessons. I wish it were otherwise. But only through passing through these difficulties will the soul of man emerge again to its true state of being. Perhaps that is not what you wanted to hear?"

Questioner: "Well, it just makes me sad really that man is so ignorant."

White Feather: "Well of course you, my friend are fortunate that you have acquired the spiritual knowledge to accompany your intellectual development and that is what the great majority in your world have not yet acquired."

Q: "With the recent events in the USA why is it that they only think of God at those times and not at other times?"

White Feather: "Because son, as I said earlier, when one is in the midst of pain and suffering, when there seems no way out and no answers, it is an in-built quality, because you ARE spirit, you ARE God in actual fact. You are spirit and it is that inner essence, the reality of the self which comes to the surface and it is pain which is the instigator of that. It is pain which brings about the rising to the surface of that awareness of God and every individual has that knowledge and awareness because you ARE God, you ARE the Great Spirit. It is only religion, it is only the world of matter with its many complex belief systems which get in the way. And sometimes you know, you find that we have to work through that. Sometimes, if I can give you an example; an individual will be in the midst of suffering and they turn to God and they say 'I have seen God, I have felt God'. They have not SEEN God, because God is not an individual, but they have touched God. They have touched that inner energy, that inner self which is the real self and they have personified it. And it is the same with all of the religions. With the Hindu, with the Muslim, with the Catholic, with the Protestant....which ever religion you want to take.....they personify God and they put their own labels upon him. But in essence, if you look beyond that it is all the same. It is all the reality of the inner self. Do you understand that? But it is pain that brings that out. It is the crucible, if you like, that encloses our understanding."

At this juncture the hall fell silent, with many of those present considering the implications of all that the spirit helper had said. Sensing that perhaps proceedings were coming to a close Amanda, as ever keeping a watchful eye on both medium and guide enquired of the audience if there were any further questions at which point White Feather intervened:

White Feather: "Where is the 'still small voice that wishes to ask a question but dares not?"

Q: "What is happening in the world today, in the universe? Am I right in thinking that many believe that God is a warrior and that is what this is all about?"

White Feather: "As I said earlier son, there are many who believe that God is on their side. It is said 'God bless America'...... 'Allah is with us'. God does not take sides. God is not red or yellow or black or white. God is not a Muslim or an American or any other nationality. The Great Spirit IS the Great Spirit and is as much within the one as the other. The Great Spirit is within the highest of the high and the lowest of the low. The most despotic mind in your world has the Great Spirit within it as does the most evolved soul. We are not interested in sides. It is humanity that seeks to win the favours of Gods. It is what is within that matters, not what one says. If one utters the cry 'God is with us' it makes not one iota of difference because God does not take sides. God is within everyone and everything and it is only when humanity can learn that lesson, and that can only come through education, through bringing about an awareness of the true nature of life, will anything change upon your world.

You know, I have been asked many times whether your world will one day be a place of great peace and harmony, where humanity will live together....a kind of Garden of Eden......and I always say that, that is not its true purpose, although I wish that it were so. This is a training ground. This earth of yours is here for the soul and the spirit to gain experience and whilst it would be wonderful if all of life could live in harmony, one has to say that the divisions which have separated man's thinking from nation to nation and which are perpetrated from generation to generation have become the rocks upon which his spirit is dashed. Only when this can be broken down, and it will take a lot of doing, can things change. As things are at the moment, you have to accept that there is this division of thought and try as best as you can to step out of it, to remain away from it. I know that is difficult but you can do that by entering into the inner temple and linking with the higher self and those that work with you. In that way perhaps, you can obtain some protection and insight that otherwise you could not. Do you see that?"

Questioner: "Yes..........."

White Feather: "But.......?"

Questioner: "But it seems strange that the perpetrators are still fighting in the name of God. Many individuals are still being shielded. There are many who 'get away with it' and many who are punished for things they haven't done."

White Feather: "It's a great paradox isn't it? But let me ask you a question; do you think that those who are the perpetrators of these acts.....to use your language 'get away with it?'

Questioner: "No.....I suppose not."

White Feather: "Therein lies your answer."

52

Questioner: "Yes, but I still find it so difficult that innocent people have to suffer for the actions of others."

White Feather: "Yes, but you know, the soul is aware of that and let me say to you that for all the suffering that the innocent have to undergo, there is compensation because the soul grows as a result of it. Nothing is ever wasted or lost. Every act is known, every deed is known and everything that happens is indelibly registered upon the soul. You cannot cheat the law. It cannot be abrogated, it cannot be transgressed. You can paint a picture, you can wear a mask, you can say that you are this or that but you cannot hide from the spirit because the spirit is as it is and everyone that under-takes an act in your world, whether it is an act of ignorance, anger or greed, selfishness or violence, or whether it is an act of altruism, love or kindness, registers that act upon their being and they automatically, through the operation of natural law, are compensated or retributed and find themselves where they have placed themselves, be it on the highest mountain or the deepest valley.

That justice is not done in your world. The scales are not balanced upon your earth. But in eternity they are balanced to perfection, never forget that."

Whatever the reader's own thoughts concerning the many changes now being inflicted upon us, through wars, conflicts and the continued erosion of our civil liberties, one cannot help but think that whoever are the perpetrators of these agendas must have a great deal still to learn. For no war, no suppression of movement or freedom and no attempt to control the thought and actions of the human spirit can ever truly succeed. Even though you can imprison a body and influence a mind you cannot enslave the soul, and the eternal spirit will never capitulate to the will of material man. As White Feather and many spirit guides before him have stated on so many occasions, 'spirit is master and matter is servant'. Let us never lose sight of that reality.

*"It was at birth that I died,
and it will be upon my deathbed
that I am born."*

Chapter 5
Return Journey

White Feather and the controversial topic of reincarnation never seem to be very far apart. Indeed, the guide has commented on more than one occasion that he enjoys speaking on the subject even though in some Spiritualist circles it seems to be taboo. Here are a selection of questions put to the spirit sage beginning with one from a concerned gentleman who was of the opinion that any return to the earth was a retrograde step:

Q: *"Reincarnation.....is it a step backward? We come to this earth to learn and experience. When we move to the higher world we progress, it seems to me that when we then reincarnate we take a step back!"*

White Feather: "You know, when you have a plant..... a flower or a bush growing in your garden, do you ever prune it back in order that it may grow to be something greater than it is? because that in a sense is what reincarnation often entails. Let me say that there is in my view, no going back. All progress is an upward trend from the lower to the higher, from captivity to freedom. The reason that you are often reintroduced into the body of matter through what is termed reincarnation is not to take a backward step but to actually in fact propel you forward and give you a greater impetus because you come into form, you come into a body.....the male and female....because you are imperfect, as are we all. We create situations that carry with them a Karmic debt. We make mistakes, we stumble, we fall, we err and that which has been created, that which has often created suffering either to itself or to others creates a pattern which has to outwork itself. So you have to come back, to be reintroduced into the body of matter to put right that which was wrong. To cancel out the debt and so advance your spiritual growth.

So it is not a backward step in actual fact, it is an opportunity to redress the balance, to restore harmony, to continue your progress in an upward vein in my world. Do you understand that? Do you agree with it?"

Questioner: "Yes."

White Feather: "I hope that helps you. Good."

Q: "When we look around we hear so much about reincarnation, are there any other worlds or do we have to return to this world? Do we have a choice of whether or not to reincarnate?"

White Feather: "In a simple one word answer, yes. Let me say that language is very important and you do not HAVE to return in the sense that you are compelled to or are instructed to by someone or by God. It is a matter for your own conscience, for your own soul, but it comes about when there is a realisation that you can no longer progress in my world without perhaps learning lessons in the physical plane of life and putting right that which you have done wrong, creating an imbalance in the past and now going back to create a balance. And so you choose......and it is a self choice, to return again to this play in order to redress the balance and to then continue to progress upward.

You do not have to come back always over a period to the same planet. There are other worlds that you can experience upon, but the point that you have to remember is that if you created an imbalance in this place, then what better place to return to correct it? And when that has been accomplished then you can move on to other experiences and other worlds. Life is endless. You think of time and you think perhaps of three dimensions, but your life upon this earth is but a speck. It is but the blink of an eye compared to eternity and you come time and time again through different forms to different worlds if it is appropriate that you should do so in order to further your spiritual education. Let me just say in conclusion to this that there will be a time when you no longer return to the physical universe because there is no purpose served by your lessons, so to speak, and you can continue your progress and learning in the spiritual realms of which there are innumerable levels."

Q: *"If we all reincarnate, who is it that mediums are speaking to? If my father who was not very nice speaks through a medium what happens then?"*

White Feather: "Who is it that mediums are speaking to? Do you mean the guide or the instrument who speaks through the medium?"

Questioner: *"If my father has reincarnated upon the earth, how can I speak to him? What if he comes back before I die? How will I ever recognise him? A medium once gave me a message that he had reincarnated, how can this be true?"*

White Feather: "It doesn't quite work like that! There are laws that operate, devised by mind that is greater than you or I. And let me say that once a cycle has been embarked upon, it has to outwork itself before another one begins. If I can open this up to you in the broadest sense......where you have an instance of a father or mother, a brother or sister, or a child that is in my world now, you will find that they will not reincarnate until you have served your time upon the earth and passed into my world. It would be a great shock to the soul, it would be a great shock to you if upon passing into my world you found that your beloved was not there waiting for you, that they had gone again into another form. That is not the way of the Great Spirit. Only when the harvest is gathered in, when the laws and the cycles have outworked themselves can any individual have earned the right to reincarnate upon your world. Does that help you?
So if you have a communication from your father and it is a genuine one, then you can rest assured that he is still in my world!"

Whenever reincarnation is discussed there are always questions regarding 'past lives' and whether or not we can access these either through becoming aware of them as we progress or through hypnotic regression:

Q: *"Regarding reincarnation.....if you believe you have been reincarnated and have memories of such, is it a true representation of a past life?"*

White Feather: "There is a chance, I wouldn't like to put a percentage on it because everyone is different and some have greater insight and perception into past lives, whilst others have a vivid imagination! There are reasons why you are not always able to gain access to past lives. It is a protective mechanism for one thing and I have to be careful here because the one through whom I speak **[Robert]** and the one with whom he links **[Amanda]** are often asked to regress individuals through the use of hypnosis.....and I have to say that it is something with which I do not always agree.

There are however, times when individuals do gain access to their past and when you have earned the right to know then it is indeed possible that you have awareness of past lives, that you have glimpses of the past, and it is up to you as to whether you pursue that to any great level. But I must warn you that sometimes you know, it is not wise to know all that you have been in the past because you are not spiritually ready or strong enough to have that knowledge. There are even those in my world......you know, when you pass into my world at death you are not always, indeed seldom aware of past lives. It is only when you have grown spiritually and have the strength that you become aware of the other facets of the diamond, of that which you are and that which you have been."

On another trance evening the guide was again asked about the use of hypnosis to uncover past lives and went into greater detail of why he believed that although it could be effective, it should only be used sparingly:

White Feather: "........I am not greatly in favour of the use of hypnosis for regression although even I must concede that at times it has been used to great effect and can be so when there is a need to release a blockage that is causing a disturbance in this life and that perhaps had a cause, as is very often the case, in a past life. The danger or the difficulty as I perceive it is that it is not always wise to look back, as it were, into a past existence unless one is ready to do so, because one can find that one is greatly shocked by what is unfolded. To use your language, it is like 'opening up a can of worms'. One has to be very careful.

Hypnosis used in the right hands by a skilled person who has in my view the right spiritual knowledge and wisdom, allied to the technical ability, can be a helpful thing. But so often, as is the trend today you will find that out of mere curiosity individuals seek to uncover their past lives, to know who they were and what they did......and very often this can lead to further difficulties and traumas. So one has to exercise caution in my view. Does that help?"

Questioner: "Yes to a point.....but are you saying that reincarnation is true, because there are some guides who dispute this?"

White Feather: "Absolutely, absolutely. Those of you who are familiar with the philosophy which I seek to bring will know that I have never wavered from the fact that reincarnation is a fact and that you do indeed......or a facet of you comes here through a physical form many, many times in order to gain experience and unfold the divinity within it. It cannot be accomplished in one lifetime."

Q: *"It is my belief that as we make our transition into the world of spirit, we become aware of your reality and that we are experiencing a part of that. When we think about guides why is it that there is a discrepancy about things?"*

White Feather: "Well in actual fact your second question is perfectly allied to the first because let me say firstly that when you find yourself in my world and no longer expressing yourself through the physical body in actual fact you do not become all-knowing and fully aware of all that is. Anyone who tells you that is doing you a great disservice. The fact is that when you pass into my world........in truth you are already in my world......but to use your language, when you pass into my world you become aware of certain things, certain truths that perhaps were not evident when you were upon the earth. Nevertheless you are still within an environment of mind that is created by the mind within you. You may find yourself in a tumult with your thoughts in the environment in which you have placed yourself and realise that within that environment, at whatever level you have placed yourself there is still a long, long way to go, a great deal of learning to accomplish and truth to unfold and that you do not, by any means know all that there is to know. This is why you will find that some guides and teachers will speak to you of reincarnation whilst others do not.

Now you might say, 'well, who is right and who is wrong?' and the fact is that even though I speak to you of reincarnation, I am only able to do so because it is something of which I am aware. There is a recognition of past lives. Other teachers, as wondrous as they are and as knowledgeable as they are cannot speak to you of reincarnation because they have not yet become aware of past existences.

Let me explain it to you in this way......and I very often use this analogy; you can look into a pool of water and you can see a little way into that pool, and you can describe perhaps, various currents and eddies and fish and plants, and rocks in that pool and you are quite right in what you are seeing and describing. Yet, another individual can see a little deeper into the pool than you and describe to you what is in the depths, what lies at the heart, the bottom of it. Who is right and who is wrong? You are both looking at the same pool and you are both speaking correctly because what you are describing is what you see and you understand. And yet, one sees further than the other. Do you understand that? That is the case with guides. We are not infallible. What we give is based upon the experience and the knowledge we have and you must question whether or not you accept it. But let me say that the greater the experience, the more understanding there is in my world, the more that knowledge can be given, and you will find that on a higher level.......and I say this in all humility........you will find that there is unanimity between the various guides who give their teachings, in that reincarnation is a fact. At other levels there is argument.....even in my world there is argument and debate as to whether it is so. Do you understand that?"

Questioner: "Yes. I find it amazing."

White Feather: "YOU find it amazing!."

Q: "What ratio of the spirit world reincarnate? Is there a balance between the number of people in the spirit world and the number of people on earth?"

White Feather: "There will always be enough bodies upon your world to incorporate those who wish to reincarnate. Of course, by the very nature of evolution the population of your world is increasing. It is a mathematical equation you will find......those of you who are interested in mathematics, that the more individuals you have, the more expansion takes place. But it is always regulated again by law and there will always be sufficient opportunities and sufficient vessels for those who wish to reintroduce themselves into the body of matter in your world. If they do not wish to do so then they will not do so. There is no compulsion you must understand.
Recognise also that there can never be a body upon your world that does not have a spirit entering into it. Sometimes it is a case that there are those forms who are choosing to reincarnate, in other words they have been through the physical world in a body of matter on more than one occasion, but they choose to return perhaps to repay a Karmic debt or to render a particular service. On the other hand there are those aspects of the spirit who are entering into the human form for the first time. This is where we have this which I term 'old souls' and 'young souls'. There are those who are entering into the physical body of humanity for the first time, recognising that they have been through other forms, or the spirit within them has come through other levels of existence. But all is ordered in a wondrous sequence that is encompassed within the perfect operation of natural law."

The next question brought a humourous response from the spirit sage when he was asked if he had any plans himself, to reincarnate!:

White Feather: "Not if I can help it! It has been suggested but I am resisting it at the moment! **[Laughter from audience]** In some cases of course, it is not a question of choice for one recognises that there is a deep need to undertake another incarnation in order to progress. At the moment I have no need to do that. I still have a great deal of course, to learn and to unfold, but my purpose at the moment is to do that from this side of the veil. To experience and to venture further into the inner realms of spirit. That may change of course. At some point in the future there may be a recognition within me of some aspect of myself that has yet to be balanced. Some aspect of negativity that has to be eradicated, and so there will be the desire and the need to return to the body of matter. At the moment I am not aware of the need to return to the physical plane because the diamond, of which we all have the diamond of the soul within us, can be polished from the spiritual realms. So I will have to wait and see."

Q: "Is there a time limit before one can reincarnate?"

White Feather: "There are no hard and fast rules. You know I have heard it said that there must be a passage of nineteen years before one is able to complete some cycle or other and return to the earth plane. What a lot of nonsense that is! You know, you have to recognise there are not hard and fast rules like that. It is dependent upon many factors, not least of which is your spiritual development. Of the lessons which are being learned and unfolded and the reasons for returning, the Karmic aspect is one which has to be considered. What is sown must be reaped.
There are some who, when death occurs and they find themselves in my world, remain in my world for perhaps a hundred of two-hundred years in your earthly measurement, before returning. There are some who return in a matter of weeks or months. It depends upon many factors."

Touching once again upon the Karmic aspect of reincarnation, White Feather explained to the next questioner why it is that some souls, having chosen to re-enter a physical body, do so for only a very short time:

Q: "You say that a soul decides to reincarnate.......but sometimes it may barely touch the earth and passes either through miscarriage or some other problem that causes death. Do such souls choose to come back yet again and experience a similar life and if so, why didn't they stay the first time?"

White Feather: "Again it is a question which I can only answer in a general way because each individuals circumstances are different. But you are right in saying that the soul, or a facet of the soul, chooses to come into a body and may touch upon your earth for only a little while before returning to my world. It does not always follow that they choose to re-enter the body of matter again into a similar circumstance. There may be many reasons why that touching upon the earth plane is so brief - not least of which is the operation of Karmic law.

There are for example......if I can speak generally.......there are those in your world who, through ignorance choose to cut their life short. Their physical span upon the earth and a cycle that should have completed itself does not, and very often you will find that this incurs a Karmic debt. It has its Karmic aspect and it is not a question of punishment or retribution, but it is a question of that soul, that facet that undertook that particular action choosing to re-enter into the body of matter to complete its previous cycle and to redress the balance.

This is why you find individuals that touch your world for a very short while. It is not the only reason, there are other reasons. For example, the operation of laws that apply and that result in certain circumstances within the womb of the mother, within the body of matter or around that body, that bring about events that occur and that prevent the spirit from completing its cycle.

You must understand that sometimes an individual may come with the intention of spending upon your world, sixty, seventy, eighty, ninety or one hundred years and after a few moments something occurs that prevents that and so they have to withdraw. In which case they may well decide to re-enter into the body of matter very quickly. So every individual circumstance has to be taken into consideration. There is not one blanket, general answer that I can give you. Do you understand that?"

Questioner: "Yes, very much so. Thank you."

Freewill is another aspect of natural spirit law that is closely allied to both Karma and reincarnation and here, in answer to a question concerning whether life is preordained, the teacher from beyond our world explains a little more about its operation:

Q: "If everyone's life is mapped out early on, is the path of freewill also mapped out beforehand?"

White Feather: "As I have said previously it is to a degree, but of course by the very nature of freewill, it is free. So one can change one's mind and whilst all things are taken into consideration and various eventualities and possibilities are built-in if you like, to the overall parameters governing that lifetime, that still cannot take into consideration the unexpected. Because freewill by its very nature, is unpredictable at times and every individual can alter the course of their life dramatically by the operation of their freewill. So it is something which, whilst it is taken into consideration, is something of an imponderable in the calculation. We can only set the broad parameters and the individual who is incarnating into the body of matter, where it has earned the right, chooses a body and a culture and a vehicle that will enable it to exercise its freewill within the overall scheme and boundaries of those parameters.

It is rather like a pendulum swinging from side to side within a given pathway but sometimes you know, when you find yourselves in a body of matter, circumstances and events can affect dramatically the way that your freewill operates and sometimes the pendulum swings way out, far beyond the boundaries of that which it should have within the original conception. And that is why, at times things do not work out as they were intended. But in another sense they are working out because it is the operation of freewill within natural law and nothing of chance, fate or accident comes into the equation. All is governed by law. It is a complex question that you ask in actual fact. If I could put it simply to answer you, I would say that we take into consideration.......an individual takes into consideration......when choosing a vehicle into which to come into the body of matter, certain parameters through which it can work, but within the operation of its freewill those can change.

I give you an example; you cannot lengthen your life on the earth, but you can shorten it. You can shorten it by the way that you live, by the food that you eat, by the activity or lack of it that you undertake, by the way that you address yourself and inter-react with others, and your environment. All those things can shorten your life and so instead of living upon the earth for eighty years, you live upon the earth for fifty years. Do you understand that? But you cannot extend it to any great degree beyond its eighty years because that is known in advance. Those are the parameters that are set. It is a very complex question and a very complex answer, but perhaps I have explained it to you in a fashion that you can understand."

Sceptics would perhaps put forward the argument that mankind HAS extended his lifespan through the advent of increased standards of hygiene, diet and advances in the fields of science and medicine. But

the point which White Feather appears to be making here is not that man CANNOT extend his earthly lifespan *per se* through these advances over a certain length of time, but that in the span of one individual's single lifetime the period spent upon the earth is known by the soul prior to incarnation and this cannot be 'lengthened' to any great degree, even through artificial means. This may appear to explain why, even with the use of life support machines, when the time to pass over is reached, an individual will do so regardless of attempts to keep the body alive.

Here on another occasion the guide explains this very point when asked the question 'Why do some souls who have reincarnated upon the earth to undertake a particular lifespan, even having undergone transplant surgery, still pass into the spirit world despite the efforts of doctors to keep them 'alive'?

White Feather: "Let me say that when, to use your language, your time to go is reached, there is nothing that will enable that life to continue, or will extend that life, not even a transplant. Let us understand my friends, why an individual passes. They do so because their body is in a state of disrepair. Very often it is because of their actions, because of the way that they have lived their life or the circumstances into which they have come that has resulted in an illness, or disharmony, or disease. Or perhaps it may be of a genetic nature. This can shorten their allotted time upon the earth. By giving a transplant it may lengthen it from the time that they WOULD have passed into my world to the time when they SHOULD have passed into my world. Do you understand that? It cannot lengthen it beyond that. It is impossible to do that. Do you understand?"

Questioner: "Yes, I think so."

White Feather: "So man gets this kind of distorted picture. He thinks that by giving a transplant he is extending the individual's life. But in actual fact he is not. It's a little like looking at the earth around you and thinking that it is flat, that it could not possibly be round. And man used to think this! It is a distorted picture. So you have to look through the eyes of the spirit."

As already illustrated within this book, not all of those questioning White Feather agree with his views. Not that this perturbs him unduly, for he always states that his opinions may or may not concur with those of his audience and that he is 'not the repository of all knowledge'. The final series of questions in this chapter then, are

from a gentleman who, whilst concurring with some of what the teacher said could not agree with his forthright views on reincarnation."

Questioner: "I understand what you are saying, but I find it difficult to accept. I as a spirit, have a spirit body now, and you are saying that I can have the choice of coming back to the earth plane at a later time.......are you saying that those conditions will be presented to me in my next life upon the earth plane in my new body?"

White Feather: "You will find that there will come a time when you will be drawn to conditions in a future life upon this earth......if it is that you are to return, and you will find that you will draw to yourself conditions that will have been created by you at some earlier stage along your pathway. Now, you may say to me 'well how can that be?' But you see, the law is magnetic in it's operation and everything that you do and say is registered and recorded upon your consciousness at some level and you automatically draw your self to similar conditions because what you sow has to be reaped. You may not wish to return to a difficulty, you may not wish to return to experience a particular pain or suffering but the fact is that you have created that. You have 'earned' that if you like It is not a punishment, as I have said. It is something which you have earned.
Never look upon Karmic law as being a punishment because always it is linked to personal responsibility. The more responsibility you have, the more enlightened you become.....the more that you have responsibility for your thoughts and actions. And if in some way you create a situation that brings harm to others, then you have to put that right. You have to do that. I don't know whether you wish to accept that or not, but it is the truth."

Questioner: "Can I just expand on that please?"

White Feather: "Please do."

Questioner: "I am spirit now and I will go to the spirit world when my physical body dies......and you are saying to me that my spirit will return at a later date if so needed, to come back to experience earth conditions again....."

White Feather: "......a facet of it, yes......never the totality of the self."

Questioner: "Ahhhhh.....that's what I don't understand......just a spark of the individual self?"

White Feather: "Absolutely."

Questioner: "So what happens to the spirit within me now......is that allowed to progress?"

White Feather: "The difficulty here is one of semantics. Of describing to you the nature of the soul within the context of earthly language. But always remember that it is never the totality of the self that comes into incarnation. The lesser cannot contain the greater. It is only a facet of the diamond. If you like.....a segment of the orange.....if that is a descriptive way that you can recognise......that comes into a physical incarnation at any time. You are never disconnected from the higher aspect, it is always there, but it does not have the same conscious expression as that facet that is manifesting through body and through mind at that time. When all the facets have experienced and if you like 'all of the harvest is gathered in', there is recognition of all the various parts and facets of the whole and there is no longer any need to return to this earthly plane because all of the lessons have been learned and the soul, that diamond which has been polished by experience can continue into the realms of light in my world. Does that help you?"

Questioner: "Yes it does help me. I could talk to you for a long, long time but I think I should let others have a chance."

White Feather: "Thank you for your questions and for your reasoning mind. That is very good."

Amanda [Chair]: "May I just say one final thing on the subject. I think you've just answered one of the questions which were written down here by someone who was too nervous to ask you directly which is 'If we do not learn, do we have to keep coming back?' but following on from that, why aren't we given a clue as to what the lessons are?"

White Feather: "Well if you knew when you came here upon the earth, every lesson that you had to learn, then by the very nature of the human condition you would I'm afraid, seek to avoid them. How often.....and how many of you would seek perhaps to place yourself in a situation that would cause you physical harm to your body? Perhaps to lose a limb or an eye? You would not. You would do all in your power, because of the nature of the human soul, to avoid such a confrontation, such an experience. And yet it may be that with the greater knowledge of the soul, that experience is the very one that brings you into a deeper understanding and allows the divinity within you to be released and awakened. So it is that when you come into the body of matter, you forget at a conscious level, the reason why you are here. But your soul does not forget. Your soul knows exactly. Your higher self knows precisely why you are here and it is that which is the guiding principle throughout your life."

"As the shoe takes upon itself the shape of the foot, and the glove the shape of the hand, so the body takes upon itself the form of the mind."

Chapter 6
DNA Debate

Some of the most vociferous debates in modern times centre around the ability of scientists to manipulate the 'building blocks' of matter. Cloning, genetic farming, DNA mapping, these and other aspects of this relatively new area of science, whilst important advances in understanding how life exists within the material universe, also bring with them a great responsibility. For man could, by tampering with life at its genetic level, irrevocably alter the fabric of creation resulting in the possible destruction of many species upon the earth. White Feather frequently addresses audiences upon this topic and here, in typical fashion he begins with an address outlining the problems which could await humanity:

White Feather: "I want to commence by just saying a few words upon a subject which I have touched upon on occasions before, but which is very relevant in the times in which you now find yourselves living upon the earth plane, and about which you are going to hear a great deal more in the days, months and years to come. For man is busy in his scientific endeavours in looking into the heart of life itself, in the physical nature, into the atom and into what he calls the 'genetic coding', the building blocks of life. There has been great speculation and reporting, upon the work of particular groups and individuals who are claiming that they will shortly be able to create life in the laboratory. That they will be able to manufacture, almost to order, life forms, to create new form and to act as God. Let me say quite simply at the outset, quite definitely that man will never, ever create life. He will not have the power. He has not, he will not and he never shall have that ability. What man can and will do is manufacture, through his tampering with genetics, different aspects of life. He will alter the genetic coding as he is doing already. A genetic coding that, let me say has been developed through countless millions of years of evolution. He will change that, but he will not create life.

Those of you who are remotely of a scientific mind or who are interested in this research will know that he is only able to change the genetic structure through taking a living cell and altering its DNA and changing it into something else, altering its course of evolution. But he cannot create life.

You must understand that life is of the spirit. It is the spirit that is the reality, matter is only the husk, the shell that is animated by the spirit. You as an individual are part of the Great Spirit that always has been and always will be. You come into form, as you have done many times before......countless times into differing forms.......in order to gain expression. And through the many vicissitudes and experiences of life through which you pass, the many things which you have to encounter to come into a place of understanding, balance and refinement, you have the purpose of life. Understand that nothing is fixed. A great philosopher once said in your world 'you cannot step into the same river twice', and you cannot. Nothing in the physical sense and the physical universe is fixed. Only the spirit is constant. The spirit comes into form and that form is subject to change and development and fluctuations. You see, man believes, or he did believe, that forms were fixed. Certainly those of a religious mind in ages gone by have taught you that God created the earth and then placed man upon it. This is not how it was. All of life in your universe has developed over a period of time as the spirit has come into it and manifested through it and with the evolution of form, has changed that form. And it has developed to the point where more and more of the spirit expression can manifest through it.

Man is not the same today as he was a hundred years ago, or even fifty years ago. The very environment in which you find yourselves is altering your genetics. The air which you breathe, which man is polluting, the water which you drink, the food that you consume......is all changing your genetics. Even the relationships and the interaction which you have with others of a similar mind or even other forms of life upon your earth is changing your genetics and that in turn, has an affect upon the spirit that manifests through it. It is the spirit that is the constant. But there is a point here which I feel I must make known to you and which your scientists, despite their intellectual prowess do not yet understand because they do not have the spiritual wisdom or the insight to understand it, and that is this: that it is the inherent nature of the spirit to seek to better itself, to unfold itself and to refine itself. Man may be able to create a new life-form in the physical sense but that life form will not remain as such because whatever aspect of spirit comes into it, to express itself through it, there will be an innate desire and purpose to develop itself into a higher form. If this were not so, then evolution would not have occurred upon your world. Man would never have emerged above the other species. He would never have evolved to the point that he has now reached. The only reason that he has is not a purely material one but because the spirit that comes into humanity, that expresses itself and individualises through man, has this innate desire and purpose to achieve attainment and unfoldment. To become one with its source which is the Great Spirit, and man will have to realise that.

The other aspect to be considered of course is that by tampering with genetics which are very strictly adhered to in terms of evolution in a natural sense, man will create an imbalance. There is what I will refer to, using your scientific language of the modern age, what is termed 'the law of chaos', where it is recognised that minute fluctuations at a sub-atomic level can produce changes on a vast scale. You cannot simply create something, even if it is within a laboratory or within a field and think that it is isolated and that it will not mutate and change into other forms affect other life-forms. That is not possible. Man must take responsibility for his actions and he must realise that if he tampers with the law in this way he will reap the consequences. He will reap what he has sown, because that is the law. Not as a result of some deity with human frailties and attributes casting a punishment upon him, it does not operate like that. The Great Spirit does not work in that way, but whatever man sows he will reap because that is the law.

You see, man has the presence of mind, he has the intellect but he does not yet possess the wisdom to know fully the consequences of his actions. So when I hear it said through those whose vested interests are commercial, who seek to obtain wealth for themselves or the organisations for which they operate then I begin to question and you you would be wise to do so also. For where motivation is monetary, where it is selfish, then you will find that it will go wrong. You will find that errors will occur and humanity will suffer as a result. So I just wish to point these things out to you and to say to you, do not believe everything you are told. Do not follow lamely like a horse being led to water or a pilgrim being promised the land of milk and honey. It does not always follow. Use your reasoning mind, use your critical mind, use the power of the spirit because you ARE spirit. You can say yes and you can say no. It is you who can sway the multitudes. It is you who have this ability. Use this ability and learn to understand the way that the laws of the spirit operate."

Q: "As we all have a certain amount of freewill, how far will genetic engineering be allowed to go?"

White Feather: "We cannot interfere with man's freewill. We can advise and assist and help him, and direct him through spiritual knowledge and understanding into using that knowledge wisely. You see, at the moment man has and is acquiring knowledge much more quickly than he is enabling his spiritual wisdom to exercise itself. His knowledge far outstrips his wisdom. As to how far that will be allowed to continue will of course be self regulatory by the operation of natural law. If man, in his ignorance tampers with the genetic coding and interferes with the operation of natural law then he will reap directly the consequences of his actions. If he learns to temper this with spiritual insight, knowledge and wisdom, perhaps the course of events that are at the moment unfolding, will change. It will regulate itself. For what you sow, you reap. What is given forth is always that which is directly proportional to that which is received."

On one occasion a gentleman asked the question of whether the soul would be affected if it entered into a 'cloned' human body:

White Feather: " ....we do not agree with cloning because it is tampering with the law even though in some instances the motive may be a good one. As to affecting the soul of that cloned human form, recognise that this will demonstrate a very, very important thing; that you may be able to copy the physical form but you cannot copy the soul and the spirit. You can look at a field of daffodils and to you and to your eye they all look the same. And yet each one is different.
Have you ever encountered what you call 'twins'? Identical individuals? They have many similarities, not only in form but in thought and action. And yet they are different. They are unique because the spirit within them is an individualised spirit. When the spirit links at the moment of conception, it is individualised. Understand that. So you can clone the body but you cannot clone the soul. And this will demonstrate further to humanity the distinct difference and realisation that man is not matter, man is spirit. Spirit is king, matter is servant."

Q: "Will some spirits then, choose to enter these cloned bodies?"

White Feather: "Absolutely. Because where there is life there is spirit. Where there is spirit there is life. There is no life forgotten, however insignificant, even though some in your world may choose to sweep it under the carpet and forget that it ever existed. It is still life, it is still spirit. You must understand that. What I will say to you is that as the soul unfolds and advances, the more choice that it has. The more freewill that it can exercise over the body of matter into which it incarnates. Is that clear to you?"

Questioner: "Yes."

White Feather **[sensing that there was another question]** "What else have you to ask?"

Questioner: "Would that same principle apply to 'designer babies' with certain attributes? Would that attract a certain enlightened soul? I'm thinking particularly about mediums?"

White Feather: "Not necessarily. You see, man is, as I said earlier, tampering with the genetics that will enable him to indeed design certain features and aspects, even though he will reap the consequences of this. As to whether that attracts an enlightened soul, I would doubt it, although again we speak only in general terms. But you must recognise that an enlightened soul is more likely to choose a vessel that will enable it to undertake a particular lesson or render a particular service to humanity. That is why enlightened souls return to your world. The reason why you have mediums is that the soul that has chosen to manifest through that personality knows that, that body is constructed in a certain way as a particular constitution of physical, etheric and astral matter, that enables mediumship to occur. Do you understand that?"

Questioner: "Yes, thank you."

The subject of genetically modified crops, which White Feather had briefly touched upon prompted another questioner to ask for further comment from the spirit teacher, who emphasised that there would be 'new diseases' afflicting humanity as a direct result of man's actions:

White Feather: ".....very often you will find that where there is tampering with genetics, be it human, animal or plant, it is for commercial purposes. It goes under the umbrella that it is 'beneficial to humanity' and that it will 'eradicate illness and disease'. That is to be applauded, but you will find that because man does not have sufficient knowledge and spiritual wisdom to understand fully that with which he works, he will create errors and mistakes, and what will set out to be one thing will in fact become another.

There will never be a time in your world where there is an eradication of all disease and all suffering because even now as I speak to you, you will be aware that there are conditions and diseases and viruses that have been born in your lifetime that were not there in your forefathers generations. New strains, new aspects of virus have emerged and this is because the law of nature sees that there is this balance to life. Man will never achieve immortality upon the earth through his genetic endeavours. There may be advances and indeed there will be in the prevention and eradication of certain conditions, but others will emerge. The greatest fear that we have is that through this tampering for material purposes you will find that the greed of humanity will take over and dictate the way that science develops. And that is not as it should be. It is the motive that counts and if the motive is to truly serve and to help humanity and life upon your planet then you will find that it will unfold as it should. But at the moment it is not doing so."

It is perhaps inevitable when discussing genetics, that the conversation should progress to other areas of concern which are closely allied to the wellbeing of humanity. Here, a lady enquires of the guide whether the hospitals of the future will utilise other methods of healing such as colour, and sound to bring about a restoration of health:

White Feather: "It will not be in your lifetime, although you may see the emergence of it. In fact, you are seeing the emergence of it in a very small way. Of course, there is a great deal of opposition to be faced by those who have vested interests in pushing the development of drugs for monetary gain. This is the difficulty, but it is in my view......and let me say this.......there are many in my world who are working with those in your world to bring this about.....that there will, over a period of time, be a slow change toward an emphasis in treating the person as a whole. what you term 'holistic' medicine. In recognising the various levels.....the emotional level, the mental level, the etheric level, the physical level and the spiritual level. Because all of these, when they are in harmony with each other bring health and wholeness. Where there is disease it is because one or more of these levels is out of sync and harmony with the others and when man learns to to treat the whole instead of just the part then great advances will be made, but I do not think it will be in your lifetime upon the earth."

Questioner: "Have you got a particular date in mind?"

White Feather: "Well, I have not got a particular date, but I can only look with the eyes of the spirit as far as I can see. I cannot see into infinity but I can see a little further than you in your world and I can see that......and those with whom I have contact inform me........that there will in the future be a more holistic approach. But not yet, because man has to learn the lessons that are being learned at his cost by the consequences of his actions in the present time. When he has learned those lessons and moved beyond the need to control by false methods, when he has learned to appreciate the whole then this change will come about. If you want a time......I would look into the middle of your next century."

Questioner: "Maybe I will be lucky to come back and see it!"

White Feather: "That will be your choice."

There are without doubt, enormous moral, social and spiritual implications for mankind to consider if he is to persist in his quest to fully understand and comprehend the physical structures of matter at it's most fundamental levels. For whilst his innate desire for discovery is certain to take him deeper into the unchartered waters of quantum physics he must surely learn to temper his unbridled enthusiasm with the wisdom of caution. He has already reached, in some areas of genetic research, the point of no return and yet shows little sign of abating his desire to alter for all time the basic components of physical creation, seemingly at a whim.
As White Feather so often points out, it is essential that spiritual understanding and wisdom keep pace with intellectual unfoldment, unless the ultimate end result is self destruction.
Countless cultures and civilisations, some perhaps more advanced than modern day man have crumbled and fallen because of their own arrogance and disregard for the power of nature. The warnings are all around us. We ignore them at our peril.

*"It is a great thing to heal the body,
and greater still to heal the mind,
yet to touch the soul is divine."*

Chapter 7
Healing Balm

The healing of mind and body can take many forms. There are those who approach it purely from the accepted medical and scientific understanding and techniques of the age, whilst others adopt a more holistic view. Preferring instead to draw upon more 'natural' remedies and therapies.

What has endured since the advent of time however, is the divine reservoir that is Spiritual Healing. This universal power belongs to no therapy, creed, faith or belief system and has flowed through count-less souls to bring relief to all manner of ailments across the centuries. Today, certain aspects of society try to claim it for them-selves by providing training schools in this discipline or that, failing to understand that true spiritual healing, whilst it can be nurtured and unfolded, is a natural gift requiring no 'faith' or 'technical instruction'. White Feather is often asked questions about the origin and operation of the healing energy, particularly from healers themselves and here in his own inimitable style he provides the answers:

Q: "Why is it necessary for us to wash our hands in between healing each patient?"

White Feather: "You know, for some it has become something of a necessity, almost bordering upon a ritual. It is not essential however. For some it is helpful in 'throwing off' conditions which may still adhere from a previous healing session with a different soul......and water itself is, by its very nature, cleansing. It not only has a physical cleansing effect but its energies upon the auric field and the etheric body can also have a cleansing effect, but it is not essential.

Let me say to you however, that I have known in the past of many healers and mediums who have toiled and laboured in the fields and have found that their hands are covered in the soil of the earth, and yet they have put them upon one and then another and another, without having recourse to cleansing them and it has not interfered with the energy in any way. Because you must remember that healing energy is from spirit, through spirit, to spirit. It is not a physical thing, do you understand that?

So in essence, it is not essential to wash your hands but it can have some beneficial effects in a minor way and not least of all in a mental way for the healer because he feels that he has cleansed himself of one before going on to another."

Q: "As a healer, I have come across a few people with whom I find the 'hackles' raise on the back of my neck! One lady in particular who had cancer and had endured a very bad twelve months.......why did I not like her? It seems to go against the healing I am giving her. Can you explain this please?"

White Feather: "In all probability, you are sensing something there within the psyche of that individual with which you are not in harmony. It may be some-thing from the past experiences upon the earth, it may be something in this lifetime but you know, very often you will find that you come into contact with people with whom you are not in harmony and in a sense, that is a little test for you. For you still have to be true to yourself and to the power of the spirit and those who work through you, and give of yourself.

You know, it is very easy to give to someone that you love. It is very easy to help someone that you like. It is not so easy to help someone that you don't like. It is not so easy to love your enemies is it? And it is not so easy to love someone with whom you feel there is something that is not quite as it should be. That is where the true love of the spirit comes into play and if you can in these circumstances still continue to serve and to help and to give, then you are truly well on the way to being a great soul.

As to whether the healing will work or not, that is something over which you have no control. You are, as you know, only the instrument. All that you can do is to give and if you can do that, that is all that is expected of you. But in answer to your question, I suspect that you ARE sensing something within the psyche which may be the result of past circumstances, or activities, or experiences which that individual has undergone and with which there is disharmony with your own understanding and spiritual development. Does that answer your question?"

Questioner: "Yes it does to a point.....but it does upset me at times and makes me restless. I wish that I could be more content in myself and with my work as a healer......."

White Feather: "Well you know, that is something which we all wish, myself included.......and that is as it should be. Because when you are content, when you are happy and, let us say, totally fulfilled, then there is a tendency to become stagnant. All progress of a spiritual nature is ongoing. There has to be this desire to continue, to do more, to do better, to unfold the divinity within you. That is as it should be. If there is complacency, then there is stagnation and, as I look into your heart **[the guide leant forward and gazed intently at the lady in question]** I can see that there is still a great deal of desire within you. There is a lot of progress yet to be made, but you are well upon the pathway to unfoldment......and I do not say those things to patronise or to praise, lightly. So be content with that which you are doing at the moment and as I said earlier, you cannot be other than where you are."

Q: "Can you tell me what degree putting one's hands on a person who is passing over, helps them?"

White Feather: "It depends upon many attributes. It depends much upon the state of the individual, their spiritual awareness and progress, and other factors which come into play. For example; the ability of the medium as a healer, the ability of the recipient to be able to receive the healing, whether they have earned the right, whether they are blocking it, whether they are open to it.... and all of these things contribute to the effectiveness of the healing. But let me say that where healing is directed it does help many times in a passing, a transition, into my world because very often there is struggle taking place in that the individual does not want to separate from the physical body. He wants to stay here. The consciousness wants to stay here encased within the physical body even though the higher self wishes to leave and there is this temporary struggle. Healing can help in the severance of the silver cord that joins the lower and the higher together and so help the individual make the transition into my world in a more effortless manner. So it is never, ever wasted. Do you understand that?"

Questioner: "Yes, thank you."

Q: *"Regarding healing, is it right that whilst healing one should not get messages from spirit at the same time?"*

White Feather: "You know, I have been asked this question once before and I'd like to know first of all who said that, because when you open up to the power of spirit you open up on many levels. Now, I understand in actual fact why it has been said to you, because you know, within the restrictions and restraints of your organisations, your ism's.....there has to be certain ways of going about one's work. I know that there are some who have a concern that when mediums are allowing themselves to be used as channels for healing they should not pass on messages from my world. I understand the reason why that is, but I have to say that in my world we are not bound by your restrictions and your man-made laws and it is a natural consequence of linking with my world that you may pick up, you may sense, you may be given by your guide and helpers, messages which are of a beneficial nature, to pass on. Then it is for you as individuals to use the power of discernment, to use your wisdom and decide whether or not you wish to do so. If you feel that you cannot because you are bound by the restrictions placed upon you, that is understandable. If however, you feel that you are a spirit medium, that you are receiving that which is truth and you wish to pass it on that is also a matter for your conscience, for you to decide. You must remember that it is not we who should decide whether or not to give you messages when you attune with us. It is for you to decide whether or not you pass them on and it is your responsibility. Do you understand that?
So it is a matter for you how you approach this difficulty. I cannot solve it for you."

The art of attunement, so vital in all kinds of mediumship brought the following question from a gentleman enquiring the best way to link with those in the spirit world:

Q: *"On a spiritual level as a healer, we are only channels. How can we visualise healing? Why should you see yourself giving healing and what is the best way to attune?"*

White Feather: "If you are already a healer then you are aware of how to attune. Attunement is simplicity. There are those who attune in different ways, some who like to visualise a patient or another soul with their particular complaint and they visualise it perhaps dissolving, dissipating, some bringing to it colours, others bringing to it the emotion of love. There are many ways because, as the sage once said, 'there are many paths that lead to one place'. All that I would say to you son is that if you are a healer and what you are doing is working for you, do not change it because in essence it is attunement that is the key. Simplicity is better than complexity. There is this desire you know in the hearts of some, to over-complicate the simple. I prefer to simplify the complex and spiritual healing is the link, from spirit, through spirit, to spirit. You are part of a trinity; yourself, the guides that work with you and the recipient. It is the linking together......."

Questioner: "So the healing power only comes through us?"

White Feather: "That is so. It comes through you."

Questioner: "Then why is it that I can visualise myself giving healing? I always feel that I should be seeing my spirit guides?"

White Feather: "I don't know why you should see that. There are some who see different things when they link with my world. There are some who see the guide that works with them, there are some of you who may see me at this moment, there are others who do not. It all depends on you as an individual. If it is part of the way in which you work that you see that, then go with it. If you do not then don't worry about it. Keep it simple, let it flow and if it is working for you......and you will know that it is working because you will feel within you that you are attuned and the recipient will be the benefactor of that healing and they will tell you.....then know that you are doing it right. Thank you for your question."

Q: "People who heal in trance......why are there so few who do this?"

White Feather: "Because again there is a scarcity of this type of mediumship. There is a scarcity of trance mediumship and physical mediumship, and what you are speaking of borders between the two. But let me say to you that it doesn't matter as long as the healing is effective. Whether or not it comes to one who works in that way, in a trance state, or whether it is simply absent healing or contact healing......as long as it is effective that is what matters. And the real healing you know, is not that which heals the body. There are many healers here tonight, many healers here you know, because this is I know, a healing sanctuary, and let me say to you all that the real healing is not that which heals the body, it is that which touches the soul. That is the real healing.

You can heal the body, but if the soul isn't touched then you will find that at some point, sooner or later, the healing that has been 'successful' will revert and the condition will return because the true healing is that which touches the soul and awakens it to its divine potential and allows it to become aware of itself and of the Great Spirit. Do you understand that?

There are many forms of healing also you know. Healing can be a gentle touch, a kind word, a warm embrace, a look with the eyes, listening with the ears, a kiss, a gift.....all of these things. Even a presence can be healing. And you are all healers, every single one of you. Every one of you can heal someone, you can touch someone with your presence if you choose to do so. Now isn't that a wonderful thing? Because you are all of the spirit.

Go forward from tonight and allow the healing, the natural healing of yourselves to operate. Whether you regard yourself as a healer.......I am not interested in that, not interested in labels. I am interested in what you can do as servants of the spirit. Go forward and touch souls. Don't try and convince them or sway them or alter their opinions. Listen to them, touch them with your lives. Let your light shine in their darkness and if you can touch but one soul and heal that soul at some level then I cannot put into words the gratitude of the spirit for that service rendered."

Although spiritual healing offers every creature upon the earth the opportunity to be restored to harmony and balance, the ignorance of mankind continues to perpetuate suffering across the globe in all aspects of life. Whilst diseases which emerged during the twentieth century such as Aids continue to proliferate, other seemingly 'incurable' afflictions like cancer also take their toll upon both man and beast. Here, a lady asking firstly if the spirit world has a cure for cancer and secondly if mankind is the cause of many of today's cancers draws a lengthy and somewhat damning response from the guide, aimed primarily at those whose greed and ignorance causes untold pain and grief throughout our planet:

White Feather: "Many of the cancers are linked to the chemicals sprayed upon your food, with the chemicals directly and indirectly taken in and imbibed by the physical body. It is not always what you eat, but what you have contact with, what you breathe, what you drink, what you touch. So many of the processes involved in producing goods and implements that you find in your homes are utilising chemicals which are harmful to the physical body. Although these take a long time to accumulate and even though your scientists say that it is safe to do this or safe to eat that, they do not look at the greater picture over a length of time and this is why cancer has become an epidemic in your world. Let me say that in my time upon the earth there were very few who passed through this affliction, although some did. There were very few, nowhere near the numbers that do today.

As to a cure, there are many cures, just as there are many paths that lead to one place. There are many ways of curing something, not just physically with chemicals and drugs, but spiritually with healing, emotionally and also mentally. Not only that, but there is preventative medicine which is perhaps the most powerful tool of all. The answer that I would say to you is known by some in my world, but there is not one answer, there are many answers. We do know the answer to some of the cancers that are prevalent in your world but you will say perhaps 'then why is it not given to humanity?' and there are two answers to this. Firstly, humanity must earn the right to have that knowledge and secondly, where it is given, very often it is doubted or it is misconstrued. Or it is not used in the way that it should be because of the exploitation by certain groups on society for monetary gain. There are.....I am reluctant to say it......but there are those who have a vested interest in perpetuating illness in your world and that may shock some of you but it is a fact, and until that mentality is overcome and the true spiritual qualities of humanity can be brought out then I am afraid that cancer and other illnesses of that ilk will continue to rise in your world.

We have to educate, but more than that, we have to breakdown barriers and superstitions and controls, and man must realise that the acquisition of money and wealth and prosperity of a material nature must always be secondary to true spiritual growth and understanding. It is that mentality that has to be changed. That is the real cancer I might add, that is the real cancer. Does that help you at all?"

Questioner: "Thank you."

White Feather enjoys debating issues with those who seek answers and here we find him in his element, at first answering the initial question put to him by a member of the audience and then responding to further enquiries from the same source:

Q: "I would like to ask a question about healing. Am I correct in saying that what we put into it as individuals is as good as we can be?"

White Feather: "Not totally. That is a part of it. You must understand that there are some very, very great souls in your world who desire to operate as healers and yet they are not. They do not have the constitution that enables their mediumship to unfold in that way. I know of many souls who would love nothing more dearly than to be able to operate as a spiritual channel, as yourself, to allow this great benign healing power to flow into your world. They cannot, because it is not right for them at this time. It is not on their pathway and so they must channel that love and compassion in other ways, healing in a more natural way, in the sense of material aspects. Perhaps in counselling or another therapy or even just talking or listening but not as a spiritual healer. That is the difference we need to emphasise. Just because you have the desire and the compassion it does not necessarily mean that you can be a healing channel in the accepted sense of the word."

Questioner: "To be a healer does it come down to atoms and body cells?"

White Feather: "What do you mean by 'atoms and body cells'?"

Questioner: "Well, to be a spiritual healer does Spirit need the healer to be the right kind of person?"

White Feather: "There are many things that come into it. The physical, etheric and spiritual constitution, the make up as I have already said, the desire and the compassion which is another facet and the ability to attune with my world. Remember of course that all spiritual healing comes 'from spirit, through spirit, to spirit'. It comes from my world through you as an instrument to touch the spirit body and the etheric body of the recipient. It is a spiritual process and the prerequisites of a good healer are; compassion, love, tolerance, a desire to serve and the right motive, but also the ability, through the make up of the etheric and physical body, the ability that determines whether or not we refer to them as what we call 'mediumistic'. If you are not mediumistic then even with the greatest compassion and love you cannot operate as a spiritual healer. Do you understand?"

Questioner: "So you are saying that we have to lift our vibrations so that you can use us better?"

White Feather: "The greater the attunement, if you have the ability......the greater the attunement, the greater the channel. It is the same with all forms of mediumship. Where the mind of the medium gets in the way, where the thought and the fears and the trepidation interferes with the flow of energy, there you have a cloaking down of that energy. The greater the attunement, which is the key.......the greater the attunement the greater the power of the spirit that can be made manifest through that instrument to touch souls in your world."

Questioner: "So you really heal the spirit and the healing emanates from within?"

White Feather: "No. The healing comes from the spirit planes. It comes from my world, through the spirit body of the medium to touch the spirit or etheric body of the patient. It is a spiritual link."

Questioner: "And then it emanates through to the physical?"

White Feather: "And then it emanates through to the physical. You must recognise that the physical corresponds to the etheric. The healing takes place on the etheric level more often than not. When you change the etheric body you change the physical also."

The way in which White Feather often expresses himself says a lot about his spiritual advancement and wisdom. He is always gentle, but firm, patient but uncompromising, tolerant of others views but staunchly loyal and unswerving when it comes to sharing his knowledge. At times of encountering one whose understanding may be lacking he inevitably answers simply and with the greatest respect to his questioner. When the question is complex or difficult he always seeks to phrase his answer in layman's terms so that all may under- stand the point he endeavours to make. And when, as has occurred on a few occasions he encounters one who wishes to belittle his views, he never rebukes or chastises but simply answers in the only way that he knows how, with the truth. As he has been heard to say more than once 'I cannot change the truth for you', and that above all else it what endears him to the hearts of so many who listen to his wise council.

"Somewhere there is a world upon which a man is sitting, thinking that somewhere there is a world upon which a man is sitting thinking."

Chapter 8
Other Beings

The question of whether physical life exists upon worlds other than our earth is one which has intrigued mankind for centuries. Although 'aliens' are often portrayed in stereotyped fashion it seems reasonable to speculate that ours is not the only planet upon which conscious life has evolved. White Feather rarely seems to engage in a discussion without being asked questions pertaining to this subject and to the nature of the universe itself:

Q: *"Are you involved in dealings only on planet earth? Or is this a part of a much larger plan?"*

White Feather: "All of life is of the Great Spirit but that has many, many expressions. There are beings upon other planets, there are other aspects of the spirit world because if there is life on a physical planet that is somewhere in a distant galaxy then you will find that also there is a spirit world equivalent of that life. If there is a desire and a purpose and a need for us to communicate with other aspects of the Great Spirit, what you would call 'beings from another world' then we can do so, if we desire to. But you must remember that it is all part of the same whole. It is all part of the same weave. I see no separation, only in the degree of expression. There are beings upon other worlds who are more advanced than you are upon the earth. There are other worlds that are less so. But there is always ample opportunity to get the knowledge and the answers we require from those with whom we touch in this aspect of our spirit world because there are great advanced souls with whom we link, where the answers to many of life's questions can be found. Does that help you at all?"

Questioner: "Thank you. Can I also ask you.....did God create all of these worlds and did He exist before their creation?"

White Feather: " I think it was the Nazarene who said 'before He was, I am' or words to that effect. What was meant by that was that the Great Spirit has always been. The spirit did not come about with the creation of matter. Spirit existed before matter and spirit condensed to create matter. Do you understand that? Time did not commence with the creation of matter at what your scientists refer to as the 'Big Bang'. Time existed before that and the universe was created 'within' time. It was an event 'within' time and you will find that, if you are of a scientific mind, and if you have the time to look into the discoveries of sub-atomic scientists who have looked into the heart of matter itself, into the atom and the sub-atomic particles of the atom, you will find that matter is constantly being created. It is coming in to being and going out of being......coming back and forth like this, rather like the cells of your body which 'die' and are replaced, and scientists have found by looking through their powerful microscopes that the tiniest elemental particles, which are indeed not particles but just vibrations of energy, seem to blink into existence out of nowhere and then disappear again. Where do they come from? Where does matter come from? Was all matter created at the moment of the 'Big Bang' at the beginning of the physical universe as it is now known? Or did it exist before that? Or is it still being created?

What is matter? Matter is essentially emptiness. Even the atom is not a physical particle. It is an energy, it has a pattern and you will find that what is termed 'matter' is actually a condensation of etheric substance. It is, shall we say......if we could draw a line or veil, if you could imagine a thin veil.....you would find that above that is etheric or spirit matter, and below that is physical matter, and when the spirit matter......because remember that my body is as 'physical' as yours and is made up of atoms and molecules just as yours is, but on a higher frequency.......passes through that veil it ceases to be spiritual or etheric matter, it becomes 'physical' matter and registers upon your level. It can be seen and perhaps touched and registered by you. Do you understand that? So it is a very complex question in actual fact and I hope I haven't confused you further but it is one which I cannot give a simple answer to. Thank you."

Questioner: "Thank you."

On a separate occasion the spirit ambassador was once more asked about the nature and form of alien life and stressed again the fact that all life, whatever its origin, is part of a universal whole:

Q: "We often hear of people reporting seeing craft in the sky and speaking of other forms of life visiting the earth. What are your thoughts on this and would their purpose be positive of negative?"

White Feather: "You must recognise that the universe is filled, it is teaming with life because the Great Spirit exists throughout the universe. The Great Spirit IS the universe. It does not always follow that it has the same physical expression as humanity. There are indeed those who visit your world and have done since time immemorial and will continue to do so. Some of these individuals and collectives are of a benign nature, others are not. But you must recognise that there are certain facts that are not available to you, kept from you by those who wish to keep them secret for their own ends and purposes.

Do not be shocked when I say to you that there are other forms of life who link with your world because it is only natural that they should. When the time is right perhaps humanity *en masse* will become aware of them and you can then work in cooperation to share each others knowledge and truth. Until that time, keep an open mind and recognise that all of life is part of the same spiritual family, whatever its expression."

The next question came from a lady who seemed to be a keen advocate of communicating with 'alien beings'. White Feather however, whilst already having outlined the possibilities of such contact endeavoured to introduce a note of caution into the debate:

Q: "In the group in which I sit, they are opening up channels to other dimensions, other worlds. How can we best attune to these levels and learn from them?"

White Feather: "What do you mean by 'channels to other dimensions'? Are you referring to other planes in my world, or other energies and other beings in your physical universe?"

Questioner: "In the physical universe."

White Feather: "You mean alien races?"

Questioner: "Yes."

White Feather: "Again you know one has to, if I may offer a word of caution, temper the desire to communicate with common sense and with your reasoning mind. What concerns me is that even though communication with other races is indeed possible, it is not always advisable and one has to be very careful where one opens one's heart and mind and being and into which one attunes oneself.

Let me say, and this may not be the answer that you want to hear, but in my world you have available, minds who can equip you with all the knowledge and understanding and truth that is necessary for your unfoldment. There are many places one can go to get a drink of water, many pools, many oceans, many rivers, but you are in my world, tapping into the great ocean of spirit wherein lie all answers. If you want to go to other 'pools' then that is for you to decide, but do not think for one moment that they will have the clarity of the great ocean of spirit. What you must utilise is your reasoning mind and your experiences as a medium and as an intelligent, thinking person. Use your rational, reasoning mind and use your common sense. Always balance this in all aspects of what you seek to do. I do not say 'do not look there, look only here'. Look there if you choose to. What I AM saying to you is that in your spiritual connections with my world you have available all that you need to unfold the divine potential within you. Do you understand that? I don't know if that has helped you very much?"

Questioner: "Not really. All I understand is that the source from which we have received the communications is from a planet outside of our galaxy and that the message for mankind is very profound."

White Feather: "But have you questioned from whence it comes? For it's authenticity? Has that been proven to you?"

Questioner: "Well, one communication said that it came from a planet within the star cluster known as the Pleiades."

White Feather: "Let me say this to you......and again take it in the light in which it is given, the love in which it is given. There are many races of life throughout the universe and there are many beings in the physical universe and the spiritual universe. Some are of the same desire to unfold as you are, others are not. There are some who deceive, there are some who wish to deceive humanity and they work as a collective whole to do this. Whilst I am not suggesting that this is the case, one must always be aware that when one opens a channel, this is a possibility.

There are others however, who are like yourselves, upon a spiritual pathway, races not dissimilar to humanity, and it is possible if you are of a mind, to attune to them. They can give you knowledge and understanding but remember that they are also upon a pathway of unfoldment. They are also like humanity, experiencing life in the physical universe and even though they may appear to be more knowledgeable than humanity, they are still upon the same pathway. Do you understand that? They are still learning, and what I am saying to you is, by all means listen to them if you can attune to them.......listen to what they are saying to you, to the knowledge that they seek to impart to you, but remember that even they do not have access to the knowledge available to those in my world because they are also bound by the laws of the physical universe and its experiences.

If you go to the source, you cannot go any higher than that. You cannot go any higher than appealing to the Great Spirit and those who are his ambassadors. Do you understand that? That would always be my first choice. If you wish to go through other pathways that is entirely your prerogative and one can learn a great deal from it. Always seek to balance caution with the desire to learn and to serve. If you can do that and if your motive is right then you will come to no harm. But just question, that is all I am saying. Do not accept anything unless it is proven to be beyond doubt, beyond reasonable doubt that it is true. Even what I say to you, if you cannot accept it and prove it......our appeal is to your reasoning mind.....if you wish to reject it, if you feel it is not genuine or right, then reject it. Do not believe it simply because White Feather tells you it is so. Do you understand that?

I hope that has helped you in some way, but I feel that there are still more questions in your heart than answers."

Q: "What existed before life on earth?"

White Feather: "What do you think?"

Questioner: "God."

White Feather: "I think you are right! The Great Spirit is not confined to a tiny speck in the solar system, in a very small galaxy. The Great Spirit is life and life is abundant throughout the universe, throughout the physical universe as well as the spiritual universe as I have already stated. There is life upon other planets in different systems other than yours, many, many light years.....I think that is the term that your scientists use......many light years away from your earth. It is not necessarily the same as humanity because you must recognise that the Great Spirit is not a human. It is said that human form is created in the likeness of God, that is so, but the human body is not in the likeness of the Great Spirit because the Great Spirit is not confined to a human body. The Great Spirit comes through all bodies, through all kinds of forms and your universe, as will one day be discovered, is teeming with life."

Whilst we may think of 'alien races' when referring to non-human life forms, the subject of 'Angelic' beings is often raised by those attending White Feather gatherings. Indeed, there have been many books published by those who advocate communion with angels and other spiritual or 'elemental' forms. The spirit sage, whilst acknowledging the existence of 'nature spirits' and 'elementals' is however, more dismissive of angels in the accepted sense:

Q: "Are there angels and do they have wings?"

White Feather: "Well, you know I keep looking but I have not seen one yet! **[Laughter from audience]** Perhaps one day I will sprout them! But you know, what are often referred to as 'angels' are not necessarily so. There are two aspects to this. There are those who believe in angels because they have read about them. They are taught that they exist through their orthodox belief systems and so at times of crisis perhaps, or at times of meditation, they 'see' an angel because they expect to see an angel and the thought form created by them is drawn to them, and so they witness it.
But the other aspect to be considered is that the elemental life forms of which I have spoken to you before, that work with nature, can very often appear as angelic forms. They are of a form that is not human as you would understand it and very often those who are privileged to see these forms, these elementals, find that they are looking at something which appears to be angelic and that is very often where the confusion arises. As to angels in the truest sense of the word, I know many angels, but none of them have wings!...it's gone quiet!"

Q: "Are there such things as 'Soul Lords' are what is their purpose?"

White Feather: "What do you mean by that?"

Questioner: "My understanding of 'Soul Lord' is that they are higher entity guides."

White Feather: "It is all a question of semantics and terminology. Let me say to you that you have those who do protect you, whether or not you sit in a physical or mental development circle. You have those in your group who have responsibility because they have sufficient knowledge and power to exclude undesirable entities and put a protection around you. What label you choose to put upon them is your choice. There are those illumined souls who are very highly advanced in the higher realms of my world, who are teachers to those such as I and from whom I can learn a great deal.

You know, at the times that I am not linking with this instrument, very often at times that coincide with your festivals, during which this instrument is taking a break from his work, I can link in my world with those higher souls. Not only to regenerate and rejuvenate myself but also to learn a great deal from them and to share with them my experiences and those of my group in order to make further plans and provision for the future work, which is highly coordinated throughout your world. It is a joyous time for us to link with such souls as this. They cannot touch directly with your world. It is a reciprocal effect, like a waterfall, and we each play our part in this great scheme of life. I hope that has answered your question."

At this point Amanda in the chair, returned to a gentleman who had been mulling over the guide's earlier comments concerning 'elemental' beings, sensing that he wished to ask White Feather a question:

Q: "I am wrestling with what is, in my perception, a paradox with the simple fact of what you said earlier regarding 'elementals'. If all life forms are an expression of the Great Spirit, why is it, if I understand correctly, that elementals do not go past that particular form in their evolution and yet WE, facets of the same spirit, have gone through the mineral, animal, vegetable kingdoms and have individualised into human form? Why is it that there is this difference with the elemental and the human being?"

White Feather: "Because you will find that the expression of the spirit which is on a different evolutionary path than the human, the elemental that we are talking of, will still continue to evolve in my world just as the expression of the spirit that is on the human track will continue to develop in my world.

Development continues for both evolutionary tracks, even the elemental and the human, they both continue to develop. There are elementals in my world as there are in your world. There are humans in my world as there are in your world and both are continuing to express and develop and unfold. Do not think that an elemental is restricted to the point of being an elemental and that there is no further development and unfoldment of the spirit that works through it. It is not the case. It still continues to refine itself. Do you understand that? Does that answer your question?"

Questioner: "Almost. So it is development on a parallel?"

White Feather: "Yes, on a parallel. But it is different, it is not the same. Because the experiences which it undergoes are not the same as humanity. But nevertheless there is a parallel development.
You have heard perhaps before, that many pathways lead to one place. One can undergo similar experiences in a different context and in a different way but nevertheless bring about the same result, which is spiritual unfoldment."

Questioner: "Thank you."

At the end of every White Feather communication Amanda, who always sits to the right hand of the medium and whose quiet, yet essential and steadfast contribution to the evening's proceedings is often overlooked by those who do not understand her contribution in the employment of the energies involved, always turns to give her thanks to the guide for his work. Here, in typical fashion she offers her gratitude, only to draw a humourous response from the spirit sage whose timely intervention brings the evening to a close on a wonderfully upbeat note:

Amanda: "I would just like to thank you on behalf of everyone here tonight and to let you know that we are coming to the end of....."

White Feather: ".......you know, I thought you were going to say you were coming to the end of your tether! And you know I cannot tell you what a relief it is to know that you didn't say that! **[Audience laughter]** May I thank you all for your inquisitiveness and for your questions which have, let me say been a revelation in their depth and their quality. It is perhaps a reflection of you as individuals and collectively as a group. The energies in this of your temple are a credit to you all and attributable to your endeavours, to your aspirations, to your spirituality and to the great love that you have for my world. I hope that as I take my leave I may take a little of your energies with me and leave a little of mine with you. I thank you all and may the power, love and light of the Great Spirit be with you all until we next meet. God bless you."

" I am but a flute touching the lips of God,
and I have no music
save that which the spirit plays upon me. "

Chapter 9
Happy Medium

The term 'mediumship' covers a broad spectrum of psychic and spiritual capabilities which exhibit themselves through both animal and human existence. This chapter is devoted to those questions which encompass the various phenomena exhibited by mediumship and begins with an intriguing enquiry from an elderly lady who wished to know which aspect of consciousness, assuming as White Feather says that we have many facets, a medium actually contacts:

White Feather: "What a clever question! Of course you must understand that mediums communicate with the personality which endures beyond death. There is still however, the individuality present within that but it is never totally present. It is always a facet of it, because the whole can never express itself at any one time, it is only a part of the whole that expresses itself through that personality. When your time occurs to remove yourself from the body of matter and continue in my world you will do so in an unbroken sequence with the same personality that you have now, that will persist and endure for as long as it is necessary for it to do so. That may be a hundred years, it may be a thousand years of your earthly measurement, but should you choose to communicate with your world, with this world, then the medium through whom you link would be aware of your personality as it is NOW. Do you understand that? Does that help you?"

Questioner: "Yes, many thanks."

White Feather: "Good. Very intelligent, I must say."

Q: "Is it possible for everyone to evolve for mediumship or is it fate that enables them to do so?"

White Feather: "Well you know of course, my views on fate! As to whether you can all develop and evolve to become mediums, in my view you are all parts of the same Great Spirit and thus, you have within you the divine potential for service. Not all however, in this particular incarnation can be termed 'mediums' because in my understanding mediums are born, not created. The constitution, the make up has to be there in order for the gifts to be unfolded and developed to the point where we can utilise them to the greatest effect. But in the passage of time you will find that the latent divinity within you will express itself, will rise to the surface. Whether it is in this life, this physical existence, or whether it is in another is of no consequence. Time, in the purest sense of the word does not matter. What matters is progress and change and evolution towards a greater expression of the spirit."

Q: "I am interested in trance mediumship and in guides who come through to speak to us. What intrigues me is that they sometimes seem to be unaware of each other. Would it not be easier for them to speak together and more beneficial to do so?"

White Feather: "This is the case sometimes, although not always. But you must remember that there are two aspects to this question to be considered. One is that the guide that links with a particular instrument may not necessarily be on the same spiritual level as another, that is number one. Also, when the guide links with a medium very closely and comes into the orbit of their being.....into their auric field if you like......they are not always aware of others in my world who may be linking with other mediums at the same gathering because they are if you like, within the energies of the medium. It is rather like putting a blanket over oneself. You see, as you seek to lift your vibrations, your energies and your thoughts, so we have to cloak down ours. We have to dampen them, we have to reduce them.
You know, if I can use a metaphor it is rather like 'walking through treacle' when linking with your world. To us your world is dark, it is dismal, it is dreary

it is heavy and when we link with you we feel very often, the emotions that you have. We feel the pain that you have as a mind link. We know of your fears, your trepidation and this has an effect, and quite honestly when we are in the aura of your energies, depending upon the experience of the guide, we are not always aware of those around us in my world."

The spirit teacher went on to explain that even though guides may not always be aware of each other's activities when operating in close proximity to a medium, at a higher soul level there is complete aware-ness and a great deal of planning takes place in the ethereal realms before any genuine communication is allowed to take place:

"But let me also add, that you should never think that our world is not a world where there is a great deal of planning going on. We do not link with your world randomly, there is no such process. We are always aware at a high level of what each group is doing and we have to work in this way to orchestrate things properly. To make safeguards and provision before we can link, so that even though that may be lost at the moment of linking, we are aware of it within our higher selves. Does that answer your question?"

Questioner: "Partly. But in my personal experience, why would a spirit guide communicating through a medium in our development group be unaware of another guide seeking to work through someone else in the same group?"

White Feather: "I cannot speak for him or her personally. I am sure there was a reason, it may have been to demonstrate a particular aspect of survival. It may have been to utilise or experiment with the mediums involved in a particular way. Each guide and group has their own reasons and purposes for undertaking a particular course of action. As long as you sit with the right frame of mind, that your heart is good, that your motive is true, then learn to trust those who have your well-being and care in mind because they see and know more than you do."

Q: "How can we as individuals develop our links to spirit and become better mediums?"

White Feather: "If you are speaking of your own individual development and empowerment then by withdrawing from the material strata of life as much as possible and by.......whether it is through meditation or simply by the process of stilling the mind, attuning with my world. Attunement is the key. If you can attune and if that attunement is based upon a motive that is not selfish, but selfless, if you desire to serve, if you desire to unfold your gifts in that way then you will find that your own energies will be quickened. The vibrations will be quickened and you will be able to catch the breath of the spirit, the breeze of the spirit which before, went over your head and passed you by. You will be able to hold it and listen to it and hear it."

Continuing in his reply, White Feather then proceeded to deliver a beautiful and metaphorical explanation of how aspiring mediums might wish to approach linking with the spirit world:

"You know, I once said to someone that if you put your hands into a river and try to take hold of the water, if you try to stop the river flowing by that means it is difficult. But if you just put your hand in the water and let the water run into your hand and then gently lift out your hand, you will find that there will be some water remaining in your hand. If you try to grab it, to hold it, it drains through your fingers. But what river is not powerless to the cupped hand? What hand, if it is placed in the water in gentleness cannot lift out a portion of that river and allow it to settle within its palm? It is all a question of gentleness, you cannot force anything. Where there is force, where there is impatience, where there is a desire to serve because of self-centred beliefs and egotism, then the development is stunted and one may open up psychically but not spiritually. Where you have a psychic who has developed spiritually, there who have a great soul. So it is motive, it is learning to withdraw from the outer world to enter into the inner world and it is the desire to do so that is important.
It is the motive above all else that counts because in this way as you give so you will receive and as you send forth so you will get back."

Q: "Why is it that when a spirit guide drew close I went rigid?"

White Feather: "Because when we link with you, if you are mediumistic, as perhaps was explained to you earlier we are able to gain control of certain centres within the brain which govern the autonomic system, the nervous system and we are able to control and regulate aspects of that, one of which is movement. We do not do this to frighten you or to control and manipulate you, it is simply a question of the guide that is linking with you obtaining the necessary control and mastery over your sub-conscious in order to use your mediumship in whatever way they choose. It is a learning process for us as it is for you. Sometimes you know, you can over-compensate, you can move one way or another like a pendulum. But then you learn how to control, you have the balance. You have the pendulum in the centre and you know just how to touch the medium, just how to 'press the right buttons' and that is a process of learning, you understand. So don't be frightened or perturbed by these feelings and any others that you may get. They are a natural consequence of a spirit linking with you."

Q: "As a relative newcomer to all of this, how can I open up my mind?"

White Feather: "There are many ways to open up your mind. You can listen to what is said, you can observe, you can listen to mediums and philosophers and teachers. You can read books, you can observe and look at life itself. Look at that which is silent, it will speak to you. Look at that which is still and you will see there is movement within it. Look at a fool, you will find that in some way he has wisdom to impart to you. Look at a child, he may be a greater teacher that can teach you much.

You can learn from so many things. What is of course necessary is that you learn to put aside anything that causes your mind to rebel. Anything that says to you 'you must believe this' or 'you must adhere to this' or 'you cannot do this'. I do not believe in 'cannot's, will not's, can'ts and should's'. You have to find your own pathway and be open to all things and learn from them. Allow the power of your intellect and above all, your reasoning mind to work for you. Question, analyse and dissect everything. If you cannot accept it, reject it, throw it away. Come back to it another time. That which you can accept and you feel within your heart is the truth, allow it to be planted within you like a tiny seed that it may grow to something of beauty and fruition. But remember there are no boundaries, there are no barriers that cannot be overcome, no enemies that cannot be defeated, no battles which cannot prove victorious."

At this point the guide was heard to turn towards Amanda and utter quite loudly '.....doing very well once you have them thinking!' a humourous remark quite obviously aimed at those present and which drew a great deal of laughter from everyone in the room.

Q: "How does a person's physical health affect their mediumship? I suffer from high blood pressure, should I be attempting to work as a medium?"

White Feather: "Anything that affects the physical body can potentially have an effect upon mediumship. Let me say that the instrument through whom I speak suffers with the same complaint and I am very aware of this when using his faculties. I have to take that into consideration because there would be no point in putting his physical body at risk. So it is something of which we are aware. The endocrine system is one which is utilised more in some forms of mediumship than others. It can be more so in 'trance mediumship' as you term it and also physical mediumship where ectoplasmic energies can be employed. But you must understand, and I hope that you do, that those who work with you and who are endeavouring to develop your mediumship have, as the first priority your well-being.

We are not permitted to do anything that will harm you or cut short your physical span. That is against the law. Do you understand that?

It may restrict however, to a degree, the way in which you can be used. It can affect your mediumship in that way. But you know, it is 'swings and roundabouts', there is compensation and retribution and there are aspects which perhaps in this lifetime cannot be developed, but others can. So trust in those who work with you to know you better than you know yourself and to use your their gifts and your gifts wisely. Does that help you?"

Questioner: "Yes it does thank you."

White Feather: "Good. I feel we have spoken before."

Q: "How do I know if I have the gift and will it be taken away if I don't use it?"

White Feather: "It depends what you mean by the gift! There are many gifts. If you are referring to the gifts of the spirit then first of all to say that you have a gift implies that you have been given something, and whilst that is true it is also true that you have earned it and when you have a gift that you have earned, of the spirit, it cannot be taken away from you because it is yours. No one can take it away from you. Circumstances however, may change, that prevent that gift from expressing itself. Sometimes the circumstances are beyond our control because we cannot interfere directly with certain events in your world or with your freewill. Mediumship in particular is a rocky road. It is a road that through its unfolding............you will find that many landmarks disappear. Those who you thought would be with you for life, you leave behind. The familiar becomes the unfamiliar. Those who you considered to be your friends.......you find that they go elsewhere. It is a lonely pathway. It is a difficult one. It is one that is very often accompanied by pain and suffering, either of a physical or mental or emotional nature, or a combination of all three. And you say 'why is this? When I have reached this plateau, I have come so far and yet I cannot use the gifts? I seem to be going backwards?' Yet this is the familiar, all too familiar scenario and pathway of those who are upon the pathway of enlightenment. I wish that it were otherwise. I wish that I could lift you up, take you out of this suffering and this difficulty and say to you 'look at the greater picture'. But you know, if I refer back to an earlier question 'why is there suffering?', it is through this suffering, which may prevent the gifts from expressing themselves, that in actual fact those gifts are heightened.

If you do not cut a bush back, then it doesn't grow. You have to prune it, you have to chop it back, sometimes to almost nothing before it later blooms into something of great beauty. You must recognise that you have the gifts, that they are there within you. They are there, they are yours, you have earned them. You cannot find them taken away from you and if you find at times in your lives that you cannot operate and express them in the way that you would wish, just be patient. Nurture them and try to do your best and you will find that you will reap what you have sown. It will come again."

Later, White Feather touched once more upon the subject of why so many mediums seem to suffer in their lives and offered these words of comfort and understanding:

".......If you are a medium then you will find out very early on in your life that you are different. You will feel different. You will sense differently and you will know that there is a purpose to your life even though you may not understand it, and eventually when all things are correct then the doorway will be opened and we will touch you. You won't have to knock, it will be opened and we will reach you. It is always the same way, but let me say this also; you will find that many mediums, many, many.....if not all mediums, suffer physically, mentally and emotionally. They suffer, before they are able to be used. Why? Because you will find that suffering ennobles the spirit and it opens up the spirit. It is like the shell that has to be broken and opened up to enable the compassion, the love and the sensitivity to come out to the fore, and you will find this time and time again where mediums are suffering.

They suffer at the hands of others, through their ignorance, through their ill health or through mental torments and torture, so that their spirituality can be honed and brought to the surface. When it is they who are ready then there is no hesitation and development takes place often very swiftly and all those wonderful gifts can be utilised by the power of the spirit."

Q: "White Feather, before I ask a question I want you to know that I can see you operating through your medium. My question involves trance work. I sit in a trance development circle, how do the spirit 'controls' determine who comes through to speak? We've noticed that some people in our circle have one or two people come through, some have just one, others have a different spirit person everytime. Can you explain this?"

White Feather: "Well, firstly it's nice to know that you can see me. As to your question, it is a matter of what we can employ with each individual in the overall energy formulation of the group. Every medium, every sitter has their own attributes and brings their own qualities to that group and that affects the overall energies of the group which in turn feeds back to the individual and also affects the way in which we can touch that group and work through them.

Ours is a very ordered world and one which is ultimately absolutely fair in its operations with your world. We will employ whatever energies we can at a particular time with a particular individual within the context of that group, do you understand that? We are limited within a sense, in that we can only use what tools are available to us.

A musician cannot play a symphony upon a tin whistle, but give a musician a Stradivarious and invariably he will conjure up a wondrous melody. So we have to work steadily over a period of time to build the relationship, to establish the link. To establish that link in such an intimate fashion that we know how to employ the various control centres within the psyche of the medium. To put it in your language 'to know which buttons to press' so that we can impart whatever has to come through, whether it be clairvoyance, philosophy or healing. Does that help you at all?"

Questioner: "Yes to a degree, but why should our guides change?"

White Feather: "It depends you know, you each have several souls that link with you. They form a group, a band if you like, and it is rather like 'testing the water', testing out which one can link in the most effective way. Some groups have several guides, some have fourteen....fifteen.....twenty perhaps who seek to work through one instrument and where one will succeed another will fail. We have to have this trial and error because we also are learning even though we have a little greater knowledge than do you. We still have to learn how to work through that instrument.

When you were a child perhaps you had to learn how to walk, or how to read or how to ride a bicycle or climb a tree and you know, we have to learn how to use our instruments. So this is why you may get this changing. When this is established you will invariably find that it is restricted to one, two, or perhaps three helpers or guides who will work through that instrument dependent upon the work they have to do.

Does that explain it to you? Good question, thank you."

Q: "I have read recently that the spirit world are striving to create a new kind of 'physical energy' through which to work. They spoke of a 'green energy' can you explain what this is?"

White Feather: "Well, every energy........I don't know what they mean by a 'green energy'.......but every energy has a colour, every energy has a frequency and indeed there are those in my world who are experimenting, endeavouring to find more effective ways of communicating and bringing about what you call 'physical phenomena' in your world.

We still employ the use of ectoplasm but it is becoming more difficult. In fact it has become more difficult over the last fifty or more years due to the circumstances of human life upon your world which do not lend themselves to the employment of this form of mediumship. So we are having to adapt, but as humanity upon your earth is gaining more knowledge and awareness that everything is indeed a state of energy........there is nothing that is not energy in some form.......so in my world also we are learning. We are learning how we can employ the energies in the spirit world to touch and activate the energies in your world.

As to what you call the 'green energy', I can only think that it refers to the 'green ray' which is a particular energy in itself and that has an effect upon certain points within the body and certain elements of the etheric and spirit body of humanity. So perhaps this is what they are referring to.

But you know, we employ all kinds of methods because life does not stagnate in my world. Those who had an interest and desire to learn in your world and to invent and create and discover, still have that in my world. Knowledge does not stand still. Truth is seeking always to express itself and there is ample opportunity for us all to learn and to develop mediumship. Mediumship does not change overnight but mediumship does evolve and does change over the course of time and we must all work to that end."

As so often happens during a White Feather communication, one question inspires another and here a gentleman enquires whether the spirit world will ever be able to communicate with us without the help of mediums:

Q: "There have been various attempts to introduce other forms of contacting the spirit world. Is there ever going to be a time where your world could be contacted 'electronically' rather than through a human medium?"

White Feather: "I have been asked this question before, a long time ago and the answer I gave then is similar to the answer I will give to you now. It is a very good question. But let me say that my view has not changed even though we have made some strides and some developments towards the ends of which you speak, of being able to establish a communication between my world and your world by mechanical means and without the need for the intermediary of the medium. The results have been somewhat disappointing and limiting and I think that will continue to be so. I think that there will be some possibility but it will be a limited possibility because there is no greater way of establishing links than through the living spirit, through the medium."

Questioner: "Spirit to spirit?"

White Feather: "Absolutely. And let me say to you that in the light of the knowledge which I have at this moment in time, in the foreseeable future there will not be a device created and there will not be a time where the medium is excluded completely. And let me say this to you also; you will find that where these devices have been applied and results, limited results have come about, there has also been a mediumistic element present, even though those people did not notice that this was the case.

You can be a medium and be employed by the power of the spirit without knowing it and even those of you who are scientists and have a peculiar way of looking at things through your material senses, even here there can be employed mediumistic qualities. So I do not see that the medium will be excluded totally."

Q: "Is there sometimes a similarity between 'spirit photographs' because the person who is taking the picture or using the camera must have some form of psychic energy?"

White Feather: "That is so."

Questioner: "It might even go beyond that, but there must be that context would you agree?"

White Feather: "That is so. That is the truth, that is the point I am striving to make."

Questioner: "It's got to be a living energy."

White Feather: "That is so. All forms of life have spirit within them. Even the piece of wood or the piece of metal has spirit within it. But it is not the same quality of living energy. That is correct, and that is what we need. That is why on occasions such as this your energies and even your voices and your motive play their part. Because as you give to me so I can then react to this energy and utilise and employ it.

If I can just say briefly that those of you who are aware and know about 'physical mediumship' and who sit in a 'physical' development circle realise the need to do certain things. What do you do? You sing. When you have your services here what do you do? You sing. And it is that voice, that vibration that is so important because it is.....referring to your previous question......it is energy and energy can be changed. It can be transmuted and it can be used in by my world."

Q: *"Why is it that as developing mediums we often receive messages in the form of symbols? Why speak using symbolism when it would be better to just talk to us?"*

White Feather: "If only it was so simple. Of course yes, we have to employ at times, symbolism, but you must recognise that in my world we operate through thought and thought is very quick. It is quicker than light. It is the fastest vibration of all, but when we have to operate through a medium we have to contend with the heavy gross vibrations of matter and the physical brain.

Now the physical brain is not the mind. It is only an organ through which the mind operates, which the mind employs and it uses language and it uses pictures and it uses other facets of the five senses. The thought vibration, particularly through what you call 'clairvoyance' or mediumship, is very swift, very quick and when it 'hits' the wall of matter it is slowed down somewhat. Now, we have to employ this vibration and to do so we have to convey messages from a higher source into a lower source in a way that can be done as quickly and as simply as possible. If I can use a phrase from your world......if I can borrow it and say that 'a picture paints more than a thousand words', you may understand the difficulty that we have.

Very often we can convey something through a symbol and it is immediately picked up by the mediums own intelligence, their own consciousness, and it is there that the skill in translating that symbol into the truth that is employed and contained within it provides the key to good mediumship. Where a symbol is misinterpreted, as is sometimes the case, it is not our fault. It is a result of a mediumship which is not as developed and evolved as it should be. That is why you know, you must always continue to strive to refine it. There is no such thing as a 'developed medium'. We have to work closely with your mediums. Sometimes we make

mistakes, we make errors, because we are not perfect and we have to give the symbols which we know that the particular medium through whom we work.......their mind, with its idiosyncrasies and ways of looking at life......will interpret in the right way. We can give the same symbol to another mind and it will interpret it differently, do you understand that?
So it is this close association between the spirit in my world and the the spirit mind of the medium in your world that is so important to us."

There seems to be a general consensus that the quality of mediumship is not currently as good as it once was. White Feather, having already touched briefly upon this aspect was asked again if this was just a passing phase and if steps were being taken to try and improve the level of communications being undertaken:

White Feather: "It is difficult. We are aware of it and are taking steps in our world to try and rectify this but we can only use the instruments that we have available, just as a musician can only play the music that the instrument permits. The difficulty of course is that in your world the pace of life, the adherence to materialism, the various distractions, not to mention the pressures that are put upon individuals means that there is not always the dedication, the time and the patience, let alone the very energies available to enable the degree and the perfection of mediumship that we would like, to be obtained.
If I could offer words of guidance it would be to seek to hone mediumship. Those of you who are mediumistic should seek to hone it, not to rush, not to seek to 'want everything yesterday', but to take your time, to be honest in your approach, dedicated and always to work with your helpers. Work with your guide. If you do not have the information as you would like it then throw it back. Ask again, keep asking, keep demanding and looking for higher and higher, greater and greater and more accurate knowledge and you will find that if you work in this way with us, then we can work in this way with you. It is a two-way thing. I agree with you that the level of accuracy is not what it was, but that is due to the circumstances which I have outlined to you, but the tide ebbs and flows and you know, there are some very, very good and capable instruments operating in your world as I speak and even reincarnating into the body of matter to work in future generations.
So there will be and always have been instruments of the spirit who can help in this way."

Q: "Following on from that, what signs should we look out for in our own development and what can we do to further develop as mediums?"

White Feather: "Well you know, everyone is unique. Everyone develops in their own way and yet generally one should look for a change in awareness, in various feelings around the body, perhaps a tightness in the throat, a change in the breathing, a difference in the respiration, in the heartbeat, perhaps some of you will feel a tension here, in the solar plexus.......you may feel that your head or your body is expanding, that you cannot move your limbs. You may feel a pressure here between your eyes, you may feel a change in the heat around you or within you. All of these things are signs that you are beginning to enter into an altered state because when we link with you we have to do so by touching your aura, by coming into your auric field and into that part of your mind that enables us to obtain access to the various functions of your body. Not least of all the glandular functions, because through the glandular functions we can regulate many aspects of your body and this enables us to bring the thought flow from our world into your world and out into consciousness.

So do not be alarmed or unduly worried by changes in your physiology. Neither dwell upon them or ignore them. Just acknowledge them, let them be and you will find that as you develop they will become less, rather like when you first start to walk as a young child. You have to learn to balance and the nerves at the bottom of your feet have to continually compensate from second to second, as you wobble from side to side and you topple over.

When you learn to ride a bike you have to obtain balance. When you learn to swim you have to keep your head above water and all of these things that you have to learn to do are very difficult at first and it is the same when we touch you because we have to learn how to use you. We have to learn the various idiosyncrasies of your being, of your emotions, of your thoughts."

At this point the teacher from spirit gave those present a unique insight into how a guide operates through a medium:

"Let me give you an insight.......and I've never done this before. Let me give you an insight into what it is like when we are operating through a medium. Let me take this medium **[Robert]** as an example. When I first started to link with him many, many years ago in a 'circle', it was like stepping up against a brick wall, for his thoughts were scattered like seeds. They were all over the place. There were thoughts coming at me from every direction like someone hurling stones at me and I had to learn to deal with them. I had to learn to subdue them, to quieten the mind and when I was able to do this then I found that I encountered all sorts of fears, anxieties, worries. He was thinking to himself 'What is happening? Why am I feeling this? What is this thought? Where has that thought come from?', and all of these things.....and it was rather like a juggler trying to balance all of these balls in the air and keep everything in harmony. It was very, very difficult. I felt exasperated to the point where I felt that I needed to have two dozen pairs of hands. But eventually I learned to control. Eventually I learned to subdue and gain mastery over my instrument and what you see now is nowhere near what was available to me and what was actually happening many years ago.

It is only through knowing intimately the way that the instrument works that one can gain mastery and so bring through the artistry of the spirit and the beauty of the spirit. It takes a great deal of time.

So perhaps that gives you some idea of what we have to encounter when we link and what you can expect when you develop trance. Have patience above all and remember the most important thing of all, let your motive be right. If your motive is right, if it is selfless, if it is filled with the desire to serve, if it is filled with love then you will find that you won't go far wrong."

*" Within the constitution of Man
law and justice are possible.
In eternity, they are inevitable."*

Chapter 10
Natural Laws

"Natural law is that which is devised by the Great Spirit. In fact the Great Spirit IS the law, the law IS the Great Spirit."

With those words White Feather began to answer a question put to him from a member of the audience who wished to know a little more about God and the natural spirit laws that govern all of life:

"You can think of God if you wish as a deity having human form, or in whatever way your mind considers, but in truth the Great Spirit is beyond form. The Great Spirit is within everything that is. Whether it is complex or simple, animate or inanimate, mighty or minute, the Great Spirit is within it and operates through certain natural laws of which there are many, many aspects and it is through the operation of these natural laws that the whole of life is ordered. Were it not for natural law then the whole fabric of the universe would disintegrate. If I can give you an example......because I do not have sufficient time to speak of all the various intricacies of natural law......but if I can give you an example; If the law of cause and effect were not perfect in its operation then an individual could undertake a certain action, perhaps commit a wrong, perhaps hurt another either physically or mentally and there would be no consequences to that, and

111

you look around you and think that often, that is the case. But because of natural law, everything that is undertaken has a consequence because within each cause there is an effect and within each effect there is another cause. So in effect, what is being done by a certain individual to another is also being done to themselves because it comes back, it has a loop. Rather like an echo, you can shout your voice and a few moments later it returns to you. You escape nothing. The law cannot be abrogated, it cannot be cheated, cannot be transgressed. What you do to others, you do to yourself. Do you understand that?

If you take something from your pocket and you hold it and then loose it, it will fall to the floor. That is a natural law, but that comes under the laws of the physical domain, you see. The spiritual laws encompass the physical laws, they are greater and yet they are within, like a thread that runs through everything and without the law there could be no life, none whatsoever because the Great Spirit is perfect and the law is perfect, it cannot be any other way. Do you understand that?..........are you sure?"

Questioner: "I think so......."

White Feather: "I think you are still a little confused."

Questioner : "Its just that it is so complex and difficult to understand, such a vast subject."

White Feather: "It is indeed, it is indeed. And one can only touch upon the surface, but it is important that if you do not understand something you ask for it to be clarified. If there is something you do not understand then please say so."

Questioner: "There seem to be so many laws......how can we understand them all?"

White Feather: "Many, many. Far too many to mention in the short time available. But you see, everything has a consequence. There are so many laws, but they are all parts of other laws. The law of Karma is another law and that is far transcending the law of cause and effect. I could speak to you about the law of Karma, I could speak to you about the law of reincarnation, I could speak to you about the law of opportunity, about the law of least resistance......there are many, many things. I could speak to you of the law of opposites.......there is not sufficient time to do justice to these things, but it is good to ask the question because when you begin to ask questions then you get answers and perhaps when we have sufficient time, we can speak to you at greater length about these laws. But the guiding principle is that they are in essence of the same spirit of God, of the Great Spirit, and they are all perfect and you must recognise that if a law operates in my world, upon the soul, upon the spirit, then it also operates in your world because you are spirit here and now.

Do not think that when you pass through death you will somehow acquire a spirit body and somehow enter into the spirit world. You will not. You have a spirit body now and you are in the spirit world now. It is merely that at death the physical body is no more, leaving the spirit body to continue in its true state of being. So what is applying now will apply in my world when you are no longer in the physical body."

Q: *"Does the law operate in such a way that those who have served the spirit world as mediums progress to the higher planes more swiftly when they die?"*

White Feather: "That depends upon the state of their spiritual evolution and, if I can open this out into a broader context, it applies to all of you whether you are mediumistic, whether you are totally ignorant or whether you are enlightened. It does not matter.......what matters is that as you sow, you reap. The level to which you have evolved through your endeavours, through your service to humanity and to life upon this world, allied with the past experiences, perhaps of other lives, determines where you will find yourself.

The law operates to perfection. You cannot think that you will live a certain life shall we say, of selfishness, and expect to reap a harvest of great beauty, you cannot. You will find that very often, those who operate as mediums do so because they wish to give service and it is through service, which is the passport of the soul, that the soul progresses and very often those who have given a life or service through mediumship find themselves in the realms of great light to which they have earned the right to be there. But let me add this also; it is not always those who stand upon the platform who are the great servants. It is not always those who receive the platitudes and congratulations, plaudits and praise, who are the greatest servants of the spirit. What of those who work in the silent sanctuary? What of those who say nothing and yet give a comforting hand or a gentle touch? Are these not also the servants of the Great Spirit?"

Q: *"If we are born into a life of suffering how is the law just? Is this not injustice in operation?"*

White Feather: "Suffering ennobles the spirit. It enables the soul to grow. It is not the result of punishment by God. No-one that I know who is in the midst of suffering is experiencing that as a result of a vengeful deity. It is the result of the consequences of various interactions of natural law which more often than not stem back to ignorance on their behalf. If not in this life, then in a previous incarnation. That is not a criticism, it is merely a fact because if the soul is evolved then the suffering is less.

Suffering is there for a purpose. You suffer because there is an imbalance, there is an imperfection and it is through that suffering that one learns, one experiences, one becomes more refined, more sensitive, more aware, and very often you find that it is darkest before the dawn. That when you are in the midst of turmoil and despair, at the blackest moments in your life, something within you cries out and you find that at this point there is a turning, there is a change and you begin to move upward into the light.

How often have you, if you look back through your lives, found that it is when you are in the midst of suffering that you somehow turn and look for help and guidance and you really, really think, and you learn something? You are not always aware of it at the time. You are not always aware that you are learning a lesson at the time but when you look back, if you are truthful, you will see that at that moment you learned the greatest lessons of your life and that is why suffering occurs. Suffering is the crucible that brings about understanding. It is the shell that encloses understanding and when it opens, understanding is born. That is the purpose of suffering."

At this point it seemed that the *[disabled]* gentleman who had enquired of the guide had taken exception to White Feather's reply and he came back with another pointed question for the spirit teacher:

Q: *"So you are suggesting then that if a person is suffering it is because they have been wicked in a past life?"*

White Feather: "Not at all, not at all. It does not mean that you were a wicked person in a past life, nor does it mean that you are being punished in any way. Let me say this to you son; you have a physical body that is perhaps not as you would wish, but you have a mind and a soul that is greater than many here realise and more evolved than many here in this temple. That is fact, and you have the opportunity through this body, through this lifetime to greater enrich your soul. It does not matter to me your physical appearance, your physical body. What matters is what is in here **[White Feather points to his chest]** ....what is in your heart, what is in your mind, what is within you. I look not at your physical body, but into your eyes and into your soul and it is what is within your soul that matters. Do you understand that? That is what matters to me and it is by your soul that you are judged, not by your physical body. You have a great opportunity in this lifetime to progress greatly, spiritually, and let me say that as I look upon you and within you, that you are doing that. You are doing that and I am pleased. God bless you."

Q: *"If there are natural laws governing the operation of everything, how does this equate with our own freewill? Could you for example, give us advice which would enable us to change our course of action and would this be interfering with the functioning of our freewill? Can you interfere in the workings of the world?"*

White Feather: "Only within the auspices of natural law. You may say perhaps we could prevent a plane from falling from the sky or prevent an earthquake or some such natural event, but we are not permitted to do that because the laws that operate do not permit us to do so. Nor would we always choose to do so if we could. What we can do is give guidance and what you may refer to as a warning to those who have earned the right spiritually to have received that knowledge. It does not mean that we are selective, that we choose one above another, but where an individual has earned the right through their past lives, through their spiritual progress to have a certain knowledge at a certain point in time, then that knowledge will come to them - regardless of us, in fact. They will draw it to them. Whether or not they then act upon it is another matter. It is a matter for their freewill, but we cannot interfere in freewill. We cannot prevent wars, we cannot prevent earthquakes and volcanoes and all of the other natural 'catastrophes' as you call them.

But let me say this also; that what you may consider to be a catastrophe is nothing of the kind. It is the natural state of your planet. The condition of the universe is one of change and if you look at the greater picture, if you look at the universe, you will see that there is great violence within it. There is matter which is exploding and bursting into nebulae, and clusters of stars and whole galaxies forming and this is very violent in its activity. One could look at that and say 'How can we allow this? We must prevent it!' and yet it is the very nature of life itself. It is the spirit operating through matter to bring about life and creation and where you see a catastrophe as it is termed, and many, many lose their earthly lives because of it, try to look at the greater picture.

Death is not the end. It is not something which must always be avoided at all costs. You have to look with the eyes of the spirit. What is a death to you is a birth to us. What is an end to you is a beginning to us. What is despair to you may be joy and happiness to us - do you understand that? You have to look with the greater vision if you can. It is a more complex question than perhaps even you realise."

Questioner: "One could debate these issues forever.......particularly the point to raised about wars........."

White Feather: ".........and this is why we try through our humble means, to bring enlightenment. Man has at his disposal, weapons of awesome destruction which could obliterate many millions of lives, physical lives, upon your earth. But we have no more power to prevent that finger from pressing the button physically, than you do, because the law does not permit it. We cannot interfere in that way with man's freewill and the freewill of an individual. What we can do is try beforehand to educate, to advise, to enlighten, to enlist, to bring understanding so that, that situation does not arise and therein lies the difficulty. It is an endless battle. It is an ongoing battle that we face but it is the likes of you......and you......and you **[White Feather points around the room]** who can bring about change, because if you are enlightened then you can touch the souls of others. It is reciprocal, that's how it works."

Questioner: "I'll bet you would have liked to intervene on more than one occasion?"

White Feather: "Believe me, many times I would have liked to. Many, many times......and do not think that we are automatons, that we are robots, that we are souls without feeling and compassion who just witness the procession of human tragedy and events unfolding without feeling a thing, because we do. We feel it here, we feel the pain. I have stood many times at gravesides and wept. Not because of an individual having passed through the portal of death but because of the great ignorance and sadness that touches the hearts of those who do not know. That is the greatest sadness of all. That is what really hurts, the sadness of ignorance.

You know son, the real enemy, the REAL enemy of humanity is not the atomic bomb, not an earthquake or a flood, not a volcano, not a landslide, not any natural catastrophe. The REAL enemy is ignorance.

If in some small way you can help someone and change that ignorance into enlightenment and truth, then you have done a great, great thing, because only in doing that will you change the course of history. Something to think about."

Q: "Could you define the law of Karma for us and talk a little about it?"

White Feather: "Do you have a long time? **[Laughter from audience]** Because you know, this is a very deep subject and I cannot do it full justice in the time available, however let me say that what we refer to as Karma is the law of cause and effect in it's operation. But it is more than just cause and effect because Karma is linked to personal responsibility. As you sow, so you reap. You cannot cheat the law. You cannot abbrogate it. You cannot be separated or divorced from it because it's operation encompasses every-one and everything and that which you sow has to be reaped. That which you sow has to be fulfilled and when you think and when you act and when you speak, everything you do has a cause and an effect. Within each effect there is a cause, within each cause there is an effect and so it continues in a chain of events and when you set into motion that sequence so that the law has to outwork itself, whether it is in this lifetime or whether it is a future lifetime upon the earth, or even whether it is in my world, what is sown has to be reaped.

Now, the greater knowledge that one has, the greater responsibility that one has. Let me give you an example of the difference between cause and effect and Karma: If you have someone who has a little knowledge and understanding, who puts their hand into a fire and burns themselves, then you have the operation of cause and effect. The cause being the hand going into the flame and the effect being the skin being burned by the intense heat and the pain that results from it. That is a simple example of cause and effect. If however, that individual has knowledge and deliberately puts their hand into the fire to inflict suffering upon themselves or worse still takes the hand of another and puts it into the fire in order to inflict pain upon them, then there is not only cause and effect, but there is a Karmic aspect to be considered. Because where there is knowledge, there is responsibility and that which is done from a responsible level carries with it greater conse-quences than that which is done from ignorance. That individual would have to face the consequences of that action and so at some point, perhaps to experience a similar degree of suffering to the one which they inflicted upon the other, feel it themselves.

So you see Karma, is very, very far reaching. There are those in your world who are paying a Karmic debt from a previous lifetime upon the earth. Something which they have chosen to outwork, not because someone has created it as a form of suffering. No-one judges you, but the law operates perfectly and the scales have to be balanced, so you choose to come back, very often to the place where you have created the cause in order to redress the balance, and this is how Karmic law operates."

The next question came from a lady who seemed very concerned at the way is which nature appears so violent. White Feather, having once again referred in his reply to what may be considered by some as 'catastrophes', continued his response with a question of his own:

Q: "You have spoken about natural law, what about the laws of the jungle? Nature is quite destructive and if we are supposed to learn by example how then do we learn when nature seems so cruel? So often we see animals destroying each other and I wonder what we can learn from this?"

White Feather: "It is a very complex question you know, because were nature not 'red in tooth and claw' there would have been no evolution of the physical form upon your earth to allow the higher expression of the spirit to come into being. You have to have the lower and a certain degree of physical growth before the higher can manifest through it and learn through it. So when you see nature destroying nature, when you see animal fighting against animal and you think that it is cruel, again you have to try and look with the eyes of the spirit and see that there is indeed a law that operates at this level which is a law of evolution and which is necessary for the higher to come through.

Let me ask you a question, 'If you are aware in your world of what you call a catastrophe, perhaps an earthquake or a volcano or a tornado or a hurricane, where thousands lose their lives, do you think that it is a good thing or a bad thing? What do you think of it?"

Questioner: "I think it's something that happens in nature."

White Feather: "Exactly. You see, nature is neither good nor bad. The Great Spirit is not good or bad. The Great Spirit IS. The Great Spirit works through nature and sometimes what you consider to be a catastrophe is a triumph, what you consider to be good may be bad, what you consider to be bad may be good. It depends on the perspective from which you look and where you have these upheavals in nature, such as those which I have mentioned where many lose their lives it does not mean that it is a bad thing. It does not mean that the Great Spirit in some way is at fault for this. You have to look with the eyes of the spirit and those who are in that place at that time and who pass into my world are there because their energies have placed them there. Were their energies not right to be there, then they would not be there.

So there are many aspects, many streams, many levels of consciousness, many laws that come into play here that you have to try and sift through and understand. To become aware of why things are as they are. It is not always quite as simple, straightforward, black and white as it may appear."

What are termed 'physical laws' which relate to the known physical universe, such as for example, gravity, can offer the senses an illusion which may deceive even the most perceptive of minds. Indeed, White Feather himself has often spoken of the 'great illusion' that is the earth plane. Here, in response to a question concerning the ability of spirit people to move through 'solid' objects, the spirit sage explains in simple terms how reality is fundamentally different from what we may perceive:

White Feather: "........because you know son, as I may have pointed out earlier, nothing is solid. The chairs upon which you sit are not solid, they only appear solid because the atoms of which they are composed are more densely compacted than the atoms of your body. Your body cannot pass through them because there is a resistance there. If the atoms of your body were able to be quickened then they would pass through the atoms of the chair.

Perhaps I can illustrate this more clearly if I say to you that, if you were to go out of this room, this temple now, and you were to shout at the top of your voice very loudly, all of the people in this room would hear your voice because the sound is at a higher frequency. It is higher and it passes through the walls which are not solid. Do you understand that? What happens is that when we **[spirit]** move objects, we are able to alter their frequency of vibration. We are able to quicken it and when we quicken it we are able to move that which appears solid through that which appears to be solid and vice versa. That is how we are able to give you 'apports'. We can apport an object from our world into your world and we can apport an object from your world into our world and from your world into your world. Simply, although it is not quite as simple as I make it sound, by altering the vibratory state of something and rending that which appears to be 'solid' into a 'non-solid' state because it vibrates at a certain frequency, we can move objects through 'matter'.

If you understand quantum mechanics, some of you will be able to understand this. The object or person is able to be quickened and can pass through matter. Man will have an understanding of this one day. In fact there are some who already understand, who have a grasp of what I am speaking. Does that help you?"

Questioner: "Yes it does thank you."

White Feather: "Good. I like questions like that because it enables us to.....not simplify necessarily, but remove some of the trappings and myths that surround the 'God of Science' to which man pays homage."

Q: "I've heard of you speak of the 'Law of Opposites' and also of the 'Law of Attraction'. When you say that 'like attracts like', what are the chances of attracting the opposite?"

White Feather: "You will not attract something of the opposite unless there is a purpose for it because like always attracts like and the law of attraction, as I've said on occasions before, is also the law of repulsion. It is like a magnetic energy and as you attract, you repel. So you only draw to you that which is in harmony and attunement with you. If something of a lower nature comes to you, then it is either because you have drawn it at some level or there is a purpose, a learning experience to be obtained from it.
But let me say to you that those of you who seek to develop or work with the spirit, whose motive is good, will come to no harm because the law which operates with a wondrous precision, which cannot be abrogated or cheated in any way will ensure that like always attracts like."

Q: "Following on from that, what about the theory that if you have problems with people you are related to, it is because you have come back with them as family and friends to learn lessons?"

White Feather: "You know very often, again, it is a truth that when you reincarnate, other 'family' members do so too. They are souls that you have known in past lives and it is very often quite a natural course of events that families who have lived together, died together, are re-introduced again, are reincarnated together, sometimes in different ways and in different forms. For example, your father may choose to come into your life again as your daughter or your mother may choose to be your brother. But in essence, the individuals, the soul's are the same, because you have lived together and have created Karma together. Through your thoughts and your actions you have interwoven this tapestry of experience, this tangled web that you weave, and it has to be unravelled and so you choose to come as a 'collective' again to do that.
Let me say to you this.......and this has particular relevance to some who sit in this temple tonight; those whom you regard as your enemies are also your teachers. You would do well to remember that. Does that help you?"

Questioner: "Yes but I would like to ask another question if I may. It is this;

120

It is said that we have a 'spiritual family' who might be more important than our earthly family and who might help us with our lives. Can I have your comments on this please?"

White Feather: "Yes, but what do you mean by 'spiritual family'? The whole of life is a spiritual family. You are linked to everyone and everything that is. Everything is a spiritual family. If you are referring to 'affinities', those with whom you have a spiritual affinity because you have links with them, perhaps over many lifetimes and there is an innate desire, love and attraction between you on a soul level.......if that is what you are referring to then very often those links are retained in the physical form from lifetime to lifetime.

For example, one with whom you have established a great rapport and spiritual harmony, perhaps several lifetimes ago, may have chosen to come back with you this time, or time and time again to help you, or you to help them. Even though you will not always recognise them instantly, certainly not physically, there is a magnetic attraction and you will become aware of them at some level, in some form in your life.

How often have you had the experience of meeting someone for the first time and you feel a great warmth towards them as if you know them, as though you even love them? That is because you have linked with them and you have loved them before. It is perhaps what you are referring to when you speak of the 'spiritual family'. There are affinities. There are groups of souls who have worked together, who have lived together, who have loved together and have 'died' in the physical sense, together, and who wish to remain together. That is a wonderful concept and one that certainly is true."

At this point the spirit teacher, having previously answered a question concerning the laws governing freewill, found himself confronted with the same questioner once more. The gentleman concerned, a deep thinker, had obviously been contemplating the guide's answer to his earlier question and felt empowered to ask him another. The enquiry brought about a fascinating reply, concerning the very nature of time itself:

Q: *"What you said earlier.......if we have freewill but the future is already known by some, how can this be? It must be one or the other?"*

White Feather: "I knew someone would ask that question......and I knew it would be you! **[laughter]** It is something of a dichotomy, something of a difficulty that those in your world have with this, because on the one hand I am saying to you that there is freewill to change the future and on the other hand it appears that I am saying that the future is already known, and if that is the case then that rules out freewill because life would be preordained, and there is the difficulty. There is the *fait accompli*...... there is the problem. But it all depends upon your understanding as I have tried to explain previously, of the nature of time and I would say to you that even though you have freewill, that freewill operates upon this level. We are talking here of many, many levels of awareness and you can think of it if you will, like an upturned cone. The point that touches upon the earth plane, the point of the cone, is the time that you are experiencing now and it is at this level that you make your decisions and make, through your freewill your judgements that affect the future. But as the cone expands and we reach higher levels of being, there, there is a greater awareness and past, present and future are one.

Upon your world, upon the point of experience, the past flies in one direction, the future lies somewhere else and you are moving along that line. If I can utilise some of the knowledge of the hypnotist who sits at my side **[Amanda]** we could speak of time as like being a line that is stretched out before you and you as an individual move along it like a train upon a track. But you see, the simile is that in the higher realms there is a greater awareness and past, present and future are merged into one. It is very difficult to grasp and I struggle when using your language to express it to you fully and I know that is a difficulty, but you have to understand the nature of time........linear time as it is upon the earth, and the completeness of time as it is in the higher realms. Even Einstein through his mathematical mind told you here upon the earth that time is not the same throughout the universe. You know of his experiments I assume, where he was able to demonstrate the difference in the clock from one place to another depending upon the speed of the object, and light. It is a very complex thing. When you are speaking of time you are moving into areas that go beyond mans intellectual understanding and awareness. But let me reassure you that what I am speaking of does not conflict with freewill.

If life was preordained, then the whole fabric of the universe could not exist because it would not matter what you did, it would make no difference. You could go out and stab someone tomorrow and you wouldn't have to pay the price for it. No, it has to be allied to your freewill and what you think and do and say at this level determines your pathway. The fact that someone else on a higher level may see things is because they are seeing it from a higher level, not from this level. Time is different, do you understand that? Perhaps the best thing that I can say to you is to think about what I have said, try and think into it and understand and reason with it, perhaps then you will come into a deeper understanding. It is very difficult to condense such a deep teaching into a few moments and to put it into language that you can understand - you see my difficulty. Perhaps that has helped you in some way though?"

Questioner: "It has, yes."

White Feather: "Good. Thank you."

It is heartening to know that even evolved souls such as White Feather are only human and sometimes have difficulty expressing through our earthly language the totality of their understanding. Thoughts are after all, so much more powerful than words and even though those in the spirit world communicate with us through the power of the mind, their thoughts still have to be converted into pictures, symbols and ultimately words in order that we can understand them.

Spirit laws may be precise in their operation - we, as yet are not. But perhaps the perfection that is latent within us all will, with the unfolding of time reveal to us the true depth and extent of its beauty, allowing us to participate unfettered in the majesty of life and bringing to us a richness of treasures that are beyond measure.

Whatever our level of understanding, whatever our beliefs, whatever our creed, one thing is forever certain. We cannot fail.

*"All true understanding should be founded
upon the rocks of fact,
not upon the sands of faith."*

Chapter 11
Pot-Pourri

**There are many questions asked of White Feather which do not
necessarily fall into any of the categories already covered in this book
but which nevertheless the reader may find of interest. Here are a
selection, beginning with the topic of religion, a subject which often
leads to deep debate:**

Q: *"There have been many forms of the Bible that have been written. Which
one is the true Bible?"*

White Feather: "As a complete works I would refrain from referring to it as
a 'true Bible'. Let me say that as in many works of literature and fiction there
are truths that run throughout like threads......like golden threads if you
like.....but there are also masses of untruths and works that are pure fiction
from the mind of man, ignorant man. So you have to weigh up and
consider for yourself what you regard as being fact or fiction. There is fact
and there is fiction in the book, as there is within many such religious texts.
It is for you to decide for yourself, for your own understanding, for your own
level of awareness what you accept and what you disregard. I have no
difficulty with that. What I have a problem with are those who portray the
Bible as being the 'Word of God', because it is not and I have no qualms

and no hesitation in saying that to you. When anyone says to you 'this is the absolute, you must accept it without question', then the time to question has begun and you must decide whether you accept it or disregard it. It is a matter for your conscience."

On another occasion White Feather was again asked to comment upon texts found in the Bible and repeated his assertion of acting with caution:

Q: *"They have found a secret code in the Holy Bible giving information of various events in both the old and modern world. How accurate are these?"*

White Feather: "There is some accuracy, but let me say that you have to use your reasoning mind and I am always cautious when I hear comments made upon this because I know that.......and I have to be honest with you and say that there is a lot of distortion and inaccuracy in that book even though there are threads of truth that run through it. So it is for your reasoning mind as to whether to accept it or disregard it. There is truth to be found in part, in many things and there is truth in that book and some of it has been discovered in the code of which you speak, but again.....use your reasoning mind and do not take anything on board, do not consider it to be absolute fact unless you have thought about it, reasoned with it, tackled it from all angles and from all sides and if you feel it to be true, then accept it. If you do not then disregard it."

Speaking about the same subject later in the session the spirit guide emphasised that truth was not the sole property of Christianity or any other religion:

White Feather: "Divine revelation did not begin or end two thousand years ago. It has always been there. There have been those who have been regarded as being 'saints' or great prophets or even Gods, who are nothing more than great mediums and they are and always have been upon your earth. So there has been this flow of information. Sometimes it has been channelled and sometimes it has been camouflaged and surrounded by myth, by dogmatism, by creedalism, by religion, by all of this which has smothered it and its essence has become lost.
There are many truths which will be uncovered in your world as there always have been, but in essence, truth is simple. There will always be messengers of truth, there will be those who point the way to the future. There will be the prophets, there will be the seers, there will be the clairvo-

ants, there will be the mediums who will provide the guiding light and if you listen to them and if you listen to your own heart and what your higher self is telling you, you will find that you will always be guided correctly."

Q: *"From time to time there have been various manifestations of God upon the earth, the Ancient Ones, Jesus being one of them. Will this continue to be the case and is it not also true that man separates himself from the higher power of the spirit through his own actions caused through ignorance?"*

White Feather: "It is true that it is humanity that separates itself from its higher expression. Let me say two things: firstly, the one to whom you referred as being an expression of God, that is true, but you know you are ALL expressions of God. You are ALL God in miniature. There ARE those highly evolved teachers and souls, an aspect of which can come into your earthly world of matter from time to time - it is never the totality because there is a distinct difficulty, the lesser cannot contain the greater - so it is only a part that comes into the body of matter. But let me say this to you; your world, at whatever stage, whatever epoch, whatever time in its development and growth, is never bereft of a highly developed spiritual teacher. You may refer to them as an 'Avatar', an 'Ancient One', a 'Saint', these are only labels, but you will find that there are always several of these embodiments of the higher consciousness in the world of matter at any time. They may be thought of perhaps as 'world teachers' or 'world guides', that is a matter for conjecture, because we seek to work now not through individuals who may be elevated and placed upon pedestals, but through many. Because the mistakes that have been made in the past are that such individuals are often regarded as being 'Sons of God' and are placed out of the reach of mortal man and that is not the intention at all.

So even though there are these highly developed souls you will find that they are not widely known. They are not reported through your media. They are not recognised. They could be in this room now and you would not know of them. But they are there because they are sent to help humanity and you will find that the highest, most evolved soul is also the humblest."

Q: *"Why is it that when you get people like Lady Diana who could make a difference, they are taken? Why is it that the good always seem to die young?"*

White Feather: "Because there are many minds in your world who would seek to extinguish those flames. Do not believe everything that you are told to believe. There are many you will find who are servants of the spirit, who are the divine sparks and flames who would illuminate the dark corners and recesses of the earth, but there are those who would seek to snuff them out, who would seek to prevent them from accomplishing their work. It is a constant battle because you have to recognise that here upon the earth there are many ignorant minds, many ignorant souls and, as I have already stated, we take one step forward and another one or two steps backward. So we have to constantly wage war upon evil and upon ignorance. It is a sad fact, but true."

Q: "Do you know of John Lennon in the spirit world?"

White Feather: "Let me say son, that I do not intend to speak of individuals because as I said earlier it is the power of the spirit that is more important. But I do know the one to whom you are referring. There have been and will be many such souls who have touched upon your world and will do so in the future and you know, the spirit works in many ways. It is not only those who stand upon the platform, whose name is in lights, those who speak the great truths or utter philosophy or give messages or healing, who are the greatest servants. It is those who are also guided by the hand of the spirit in other ways. Music is a great healer. Music is a great power of the spirit. Writing, poetry, even listening........saying nothing, just listening......just being there......these are the servants of the spirit."

Questioner: "Is he still writing music in your world?"

White Feather: "When death occurs and the physical body is no more, those who have this desire to work in this way will continue to do so in my world. But the one to whom you refer still makes music, still writes, still enables the talents that he had to work in this way and without saying too much, let me say that, that individual is also working closely with one upon your world who was one half of two **[Paul McCartney?]** Do you understand that? There is still a link.......there is still a link, because when two minds work together so closely they establish more than a physical friendship. There is a spiritual link and there is still work here being done from spirit to your world of matter. There is still guidance. There is still help being given. I will say no more than that."

Q: "It is said that the end of the world is coming at the close of the 20th Century. Can you shed any light on this?"

White Feather: "Who told you that?"

Questioner: "It is written in the history books, Nostradamus told us."

White Feather: "Well you know, I don't care a great deal for history because quite frankly much of what you regard and accept as history is not true. As to the end of the world, let me say that it will not occur in your twentieth century nor will it occur in your twenty-first century! You will find that life will continue in your world, which has been in existence for a lot longer than even your scientists recognise. It will continue to exist, for that is the plan and the purpose and man, even through his ignorance, although he may strive to destroy it and indeed may be partly successful in destroying some aspects of life, life will persist because matter does not control the spirit. It is the spirit that controls matter. It is spirit that is master, it it matter that is servant. So don't worry about the end of the world, it certainly won't be in your lifetime upon it."

The so called 'Akashic Records', an absolute record of all that has ever occurred apparently exists upon the astral plane. Here, White Feather acknowledges their existence and states that we can all have access to them at some point:

Q: "The Akashic Records...do they exist and can individuals access them?"

White Feather: "You will be able to access them through your meditation and indeed in my world you will be able to visit the Halls of Learning and the Great Libraries where the true record of history is kept."

Q: "I too have read about the Akashic Records, is there knowledge gained from the collective unconscious? For example, the Red Indians had knowledge yet they could not read or write?"

White Feather: "Knowledge is drawn from many sources. The Akashic Records of which you speak are knowledge, an absolute record of everything that has ever occurred, will ever occur, upon your world and indeed within the universe and there are many forms, many groups, many individuals who have earned the right to gain access to that knowledge. Whatever means they use, whatever labelling, whatever society or group they are part of is only a means that they can utilise to achieve that knowledge and gain contact with the Akashic Records. I am not particularly concerned with the mechanism used. What is important is the fact that one can, if one has earned the right........spiritually earned the right to have an attunement with the Akashic Records, one can do so. Whether one is part of a group, a gathering, or whether one is working in an individual way, if one has earned the right spiritually, one can achieve it."

Q: "My question is about dreams. I understand that when we have a dream we release from our body but I equally wonder how that fits in with nightmares that we sometimes have?"

White Feather: Well you know, not all dreams are real experiences on the spirit planes. There are times in the sleep state where your consciousness can temporarily remove itself from its seat in the physical body, the physical brain and experience the spiritual dimension through the astral body and there you can have experiences during the sleep state which are conveyed back to you as dreams.

Very often they are vivid ones and very real to you and these are true experiences on the astral planes of life and even beyond, but sometimes what you call dreams are merely the effects of the food that you have eaten the night before, which also changes the chemistry of your body and can have an influence upon the consciousness. You see, you have to appreciate, to weigh it up and consider it. As to nightmares, you know I have to say that sometimes a nightmare, even though it can be caused by subconscious or unconscious experiences which may have frightened you, has to have a release. It is a kind of release valve that takes place. It can also be an experience that you have upon the astral plane, because the astral planes are filled with thought forms, not all of which are pleasant. They cannot hurt you, they cannot injure you either spiritually or physically but they can have a mental effect upon you.

You must recognise that there are many thought forms. Every thought that you think, has a form. In some instances if the thought is very 'light-weight'.....perhaps you are thinking of what you are going to prepare for your supper.......you will find that, that thought as it leaves your mind, disintegrates. If however, you are holding thoughts of anger, that you wish to perhaps cause grief and hurt to another and you build these thoughts up until they become so powerful that they almost take upon themselves a life of their own......... they surround you and they are released onto the astral plane......and there can be times when, during the sleep state you become aware of these thoughts, even though they are not directly linking with you, you sense them, you become aware of them and this is what transforms into a nightmare.

So you see, there is much that your world does not understand about the power of thought. Thought is so powerful. If you could see some of the clouds of thought formed over particular individuals or even nations or groups who are hell bent upon violence or oppression or hatred, you would do well to steer clear of them because they are very powerful. Equally, you can experience thought forms of a delightful nature, so it is a very complex thing. You have to determine when you wake up and you have those thoughts, a memory of that dream or nightmare......you have to stop and think, 'Is there a message in this? Is it real or is it just a product of my unconscious processes or a thought form?' Do you understand that?"

Questioner: "Yes, very much so. Thank you very much indeed."

The next question was asked at a trance evening shortly before a major eclipse of the sun was due to occur over Great Britain:

Q: "Is there a spiritual significance with the coming eclipse on August 11th?"

White Feather: "Well you know, I keep looking for one but I can't find it yet! **[Laughter from audience]** The eclipse is a natural phenomenon. Of course, everything in the universe, particularly in your solar system, has its effect, its magnetic effect upon your earth. The alignment of the planets, the movement of the planets and the sun and stars and moon and the earth, they are all part of one system and so there are certain aspects and energies to be considered. But I would not read too much into or place too much emphasis on it being something of great spiritual significance because I have yet to discover that. Unless you have something more to enlighten me with!"

Q: "We are very interested in David Icke's information in his latest book but find it confusing and bewildering. Have you any advice or counselling on this?"

White Feather: "Well let me say that there are aspects of it which I find confusing and bewildering also, because there are many points of view and information drawn from a great many places, but let me say that we are aware in my world of this man and of his work and there are those in my world who work with him.
All that I would say is that one has to apply one's own intellect and reasoning mind as well as one's spiritual intuition and understanding in reading any work, whether it is by a specific individual or a collective and however it is regarded in your world, you must use your own reasoning mind. If anything that you hear, you read or you see offends your reasoning mind then discard it, leave it, put it to one side for a little while and

perhaps then, return to it and you will find that you can either then reject it or accept it."

Questioner: "Are you saying then that you agree or disagree with his theories?"

White Feather: "Always use your ability to understand and to think and to reason because there are many things with which you will become familiar that you cannot accept because they are either too extreme or you are not yet ready to understand them. It is not my intention to elaborate or speak at any great length about individuals because that would be unfair of me. Who am I to judge or comment upon the works of others? Each seeks to work and to enable the spirit to manifest through them in their own unique ways. We are all upon the pathway of learning. We are all imperfect but there is truth to be found in many ways, in many places and from many sources. It is for you to decide whether it is correct or incorrect, whether it finds an affinity within you or whether you seek to reject it."

The humour of White Feather again shone through when he was asked what he did in his spare time!:

White Feather: "Well, I like to put my feet up and perhaps read a few books! That is of course when I am not playing my harp! But in answer to your question, which I regard with all seriousness, there is a great deal to do in my world. We have a great deal of work to undertake. I do not operate through another instrument upon this earth, one is enough! But I do have great joy in undertaking many of the activities that are abundant in my world. We have halls of great learning, libraries, halls of music......we partake in many activities in this fashion and we are never short of things to do, people to meet, friends and compatriots with whom to share the most wonderful conversations and there is plenty yet to learn.

So I am never at a loss for anything to do. There are times of course when I choose just to rest and to contemplate and to meditate and link with the Great Spirit as you do when you meditate. So life is not so different, but it is much more rich and varied and more real in many respects than is life upon your world. Does that help you?"

Questioner: "Thank you sir, thank you."

Q: "Will some spirits choose to enter 'cloned' bodies?"

White Feather: "Absolutely. Because where there is life, there is spirit. Where there is spirit, there is life. There is no life, however small, however insignificant, even though some in your world may choose to 'sweep it under the carpet and forget that it ever existed, that is not spirit. It is still life. You must understand that. What I will say to you is that as the soul unfolds and advances, the more choice that it has. The more freewill that it can exercise over the body of matter into which it incarnates. Is that clear to you?"

Questioner: "Yes."

Sensing that the lady had a further question in her mind the guide continued:

White Feather: "Good.........what else have you to ask?"

Questioner: "Would that same principle apply to designer babies with certain attributes? Would that attract a certain enlightened soul? I'm thinking particularly about mediums?"

White Feather: "Not necessarily. You see, man is tampering with genetics that will enable him to indeed, design certain features and aspects even though he will reap the consequences of this. As to whether that attracts an enlightened soul, I would doubt it, although again we can speak only in general terms. But you must recognise that an enlightened soul is more likely to choose a vessel that will enable it to undertake a particular lesson or render a particular service to humanity. That is why enlightened souls return to your world. The reason why you have mediums is that the soul that has chosen to manifest through that personality knows that, that medium is constructed in a certain way as a particular constitution of physical, etheric and astral matter, that enables 'mediumship' to occur. Do you understand that?"

The lady in question nodded in agreement and thanked the teacher for his answer. Yet so often, as has been demonstrated at trance evenings over the years, one question prompts another and here a gentleman enquires of the guide if parental choice is really an option:

Q: "Is it true that we actually choose our parents? There seems to be conflicting views upon this."

White Feather: "Yes.....again sometimes this is so, but not always. You have recognise that it is in accordance with the progress that has been made by the soul and whether or not it has earned the right to choose it's parents. Sometimes the process is more automatic in its operation, but where there has been progress made and where there is a particular lesson to be learned or specific service to be rendered then the soul has the opportunity to choose it's parentage and if it does so wisely, will enable that facet which is expressing itself in the physical body to gain the greatest benefits from that incarnation."

Q: "Following on from the last question, when we enter the spirit world do we have partial or total recall of our past lives?"

White Feather: "You do not always have total or partial recall, not immediately. You must understand that when you are free of the physical body and you are in my world you are still very much as you are now. You have created yourselves. It is only with the passage of time that a greater realisation begins to dawn within the conscious state and you become aware, either partially or completely of past experiences and past lives. This is why you have some spirit helpers and guides, such as myself, who emphasise that reincarnation is indeed a truth whilst others say that it is not. Who is right? Who is wrong? It is a matter of experience. No one is allowed to communicate in this way and to speak of something which they themselves have no knowledge of on a personal level, that they have not experienced. Even some of those helpers and guides that link with mediums in your world and have done throughout the ages of time do not speak of reincarnation because they themselves have yet to register that as a truth within their conscious understanding. Do you understand that? I speak of it because I have a knowledge of it. Were that not the case then I would not be permitted to."

Here, a question is put to White Feather from Amanda who enquires of the sage whether people with whom we find difficulty relating should be avoided:

Amanda: "When we meet someone and instinctively don't like them, is it true that these are people who should not cross our pathway in life?"

White Feather: "No, it is not so. Because you may draw to you someone whom you do not like for a very good reason. If you passed through life only meeting those whom you liked, then you would not learn all of life's lessons. As I have already stated, you have to have the dark to know the light. You have to link with the ignorant and with the foolish, with the evil often, in order to appreciate the good and the benign. You have to have the polarity in order to come into this place of balance and you will automatically draw to you that which is right for you at any time, even though consciously you may consider it to be bad or wrong. Nevertheless on a higher level you may have drawn it to you. Do you understand that? Do you agree with it? **[No answer - laughter from the audience]**

Amanda: "I think we'll move on."

White Feather: "No, I think we will stay because I feel there is a disagreement here."

Amanda: "There are some people that I have met when entering a room and I've thought 'I don't like you, I don't want anything to do with you', and I've been proven right. Other people have said to me 'You've got it wrong, they are not like that', but in time I've been proved right."

White Feather: "Of course that is so.....that is the case. I am not disputing that. Because you are sensitive then you automatically sense people with whom you do not have an affinity, but what I am saying to you is that there may well be a reason why at some level you have drawn that soul to you. Whether or not you register that dislike instantly is a matter for your own spiritual awareness because the more aware that you are, the more sensitive you are, the more likely it is that you will sense this.
So I am not disputing that at all. What you must recognise is that you often draw these individuals to you for a reason. I am glad we haven't disagreed about that!" **[Laughter from audience]**

Q: "Concerning people we don't get on with or we don't like, is it right then that although these people may be drawn to us, it is the light within them that draws them to us and actually helps them along their pathway?"

White Feather: "It is a little more complex than that but let me say that in an ordered universe which is controlled and regulated by laws and energies that work within them, there is nothing that happens by chance or fate or luck. If you meet someone then it is often, if not always, for a reason. They may be aware of it consciously, they may not. You may be aware of it consciously, you may not. But you can rest assured that at some level there is a law that is operating that has drawn you magnetically together at that point for whatever reason is applicable at the soul level."

Q: "How do we know what good and evil is? How do we know when we are dealing with it?"

White Feather: "Well I sincerely hope that you don't work with evil! But you know, everything has its opposite. To good there is evil, to light there is dark, to negative there is positive, to male there is female, to high there is low, to weak there is strong......I could go on and on. To captivity there is freedom, to love there is hatred and you as an individual come into this ocean of energies and emotions and thoughts and I would say to you that as you develop spiritually, so you learn to discern the one from the other.

So many act from selfishness, from the 'culture of want' as I refer to it, where self importance and egotism far transcends humility and the desire to serve and to me, that is a form of evil. Evil to me, is where the spirit is denied and where one seeks to impose its will upon another. Where one seeks to prevent the light and the truth from illuminating the darkness. Where one seeks to captivate another and to force them against their will into beliefs and doctrines and methods of thinking and acting that are contrary to the ways of the spirit. So evil covers a whole range of things. The greatest evil is where there is knowledge and still the individual denies it and acts in a manner contrary to it, through their own selfish egotism. That is the greatest evil of all.

As to whether you know one from the other, let me say this; there is what I call 'the compass of the soul' within each individual. It is the conscience, and even within a child there is a conscience and indeed within everyone. Whether it is the lowest of the low or whether it is the murderer or the rapist or the thief or whether it is the saint or the prophet or the healer or the great teacher......there is still a conscience within each of them and if you are honest with yourself you will know right from wrong because your conscience will tell you. The greatest evil perhaps, is where you deny it, you do not listen to it and then you will find that you are opened up to all manner of things."

Q: "Sometimes when I am going to sleep I find myself with a brilliant blue light inside my forehead. Could you explain what it is please?"

White Feather: "You know, when you begin to develop there are certain areas within the constitution of your etheric and higher spiritual bodies that become open. They may have been previously dormant or asleep and they become awakened. I do not like to use the term 'chakra'.....it is not a term I normally employ, but let me say that there are various energy centres, one of which is within the centre of your forehead, where energy is drawn to you and those guides that work with you will employ this centre of activity to further your development and open what is referred to as your 'third eye'. Now, you may see this and witness this in many ways. Very often you will find that this is in the sense of a light which you see 'clairvoyantly' and I know that is what you are experiencing.

You will find, many of you........and I talk to all of you now who are developing spiritually.......that when these centres are opened, when they are active, when you are developing nicely, you will find that you do not notice these things as much. It is when you are first developing that they are noticeable because you had not noticed them before and that centre of activity had not been employed before. As you develop you will find that you do not notice these things as much and that is as it should be, because it is a sign of your development. So just go with it. Do not be fearful of it and recognise that those who work with you have a greater knowledge of you than even you do and they are drawing to you and bringing energy to you that will assist you in your spiritual and psychic development."

Q: *"From where does the spirit body leave the physical body when death occurs?"*

White Feather: "Let me say that ultimately, it leaves through the head, the crown centre, although there are those who would disagree with this. But you must understand that it is through this centre, which is the highest centre of the constitutional make-up of the bodies of man.......it is through this centre that it makes its final exit. I have witnessed many times, individuals passing from your world into mine and you know you have heard it said perhaps yourself, that an individual........to use your language 'dies from the feet upwards', in that the spirit body withdraws from the lower extremities and finally withdraws out through the top. That is very often the case in a normal passing and those of you who have clairvoyant vision will indeed be able to witness this if you are in a position where someone passes in your presence."

Although White Feather often deals with very 'deep' questions that deal with some of the fundamental issues of creation, the reverse may also be the case. Yet here, in his own unique way he turns what appears to be a somewhat banal question into an answer that allows him to impart a more profound spiritual teaching:

Q: *"Many people in this world like to have a pint of beer. Will we still be able to have a pint in the spirit world?"*

White Feather: "It may surprise you son, but if you want to have a pint you can have a pint! It won't harm you, it won't do you any good but you can have it if you want!

If you believe you have a train to catch, it will be there waiting for you. It is all in accordance with your state of mind and spiritual development. In all seriousness, there is a greater implication behind your question because there are so many in my world who still believe, because their belief systems are so strong, so structured, so rigid, that they have to have certain things, they have to be in certain surroundings, and because their thoughts are so dynamic and so rigid, so powerful, they create that environment.

You must remember that my world is the world of thought. As you think, so you are, so you create. It is a mental plane and if you have a particular religious belief for example and you have been in the habit of going to a church religiously on a Sunday, singing the same hymns and reciting the same prayers and you believe that is what awaits you in the kingdom beyond, then there is every possibility that it will be there for you because that is your belief system. That is what you create and very often it can be a hindrance, it can be a stumbling block which has to be overcome.

Equally of course, we have those who are of a more liberated mind and they realise that there are infinite possibilities that await them. When they are in my world they can put aside all the things and all the trappings of the earthly plane, which even though they may have enjoyed, they realise they no longer need and they can go on to things of a more enjoyable nature of which there are countless examples.

So whilst I enter into the humour of your question, I also point out the seriousness of it."

Only White Feather could give an answer like that and perhaps therein lies a lesson for us all. For if the seemingly mundane can be transformed into the magical by the application of knowledge and understanding then surely even the most dour of lives can aspire to the greatness of spiritual attainment. What can be achieved by one, can be achieved by all and the only boundaries are those which we set upon ourselves.

*" Look into the depths of your being
and you will see how shallow
is your understanding."*

Chapter 12
The Voice

Primarily, this has been a book about questions and answers, with each chapter devoted to the many souls who have ventured to ask White Feather what puzzled and perplexed them, always to receive his carefully crafted answers delivered in a gentle, kind and forthright manner. Yet the guide often speaks through his medium simply to impart a teaching without recourse for questions and some of his most powerful talks have been delivered in this way. Here is an unabridged address given at Northampton Spiritualist Church. In full flow, the teacher from beyond our world gives rein to the spiritual philosophy for which he has become known and loved, beginning as always with his customary introduction to those present:

" May I greet you all with the divine light and the radiant love of the Great White Spirit. It is always a great honour and privilege to have, as I often do, this opportunity to speak with you through this instrument and I pay tribute to the wondrous operation of natural spirit law that permits me to utilise this channel in order to speak to you. Although this is a task which I have under-taken on numerous occasions it is one of which I never grow weary for there are many challenges to be faced, not only by humanity but also by those many legions of servants of the spirit in my world and not least of which is the challenge of helping and guiding humanity to climb and to ascend to the plateau of spiritual knowledge and truth. For so many in your world are tied and bound by the chattels and the chains of ignorance, dogmatism, creedalism, oppression and fear and it is only when perhaps, very often through suffering, these aspects can be challenged that the divine nature of the self which resides at the heart of you all can be brought to the surface. Then it is that liberation can be forthcoming. But it is a long, arduous and difficult journey upon which you are all engaged and I offer you all no easy solutions, no easy fixes, because you have to experience very often the dark, to know the light. You have to undergo ignorance in order to know truth and you have to have been a captive in order to discover freedom.

Let me say as I often do right at the outset, that who I am is of little consequence. I am, like you human in every regard. I have a body just as you do. I have limbs as you do, I have eyes with which to see, ears through which to hear, a mouth through which to speak and a mind through which to think. The only difference perhaps is that I no longer have the heavy encumbrance of a physical body with which to contend. I am free of that and so I am able to express far greater a reality than upon your world. That does not mean that in any way I am greater than you or better. It simply means that I have been able, through many lifetimes to gather up the experiences through which I have passed and to offer you their benefits in the form of knowledge and understanding. I still have a great deal to unfold and a great deal to learn but perhaps I can afford you the opportunity of coming into a deeper understanding yourselves tonight by what I say to do.

You know there is an old saying......I think it arose and originated in your world and it goes 'may you live in interesting times' and you certainly do live in interesting times because there is much change going on around you, great change and upheaval. You may have noticed the changes in your weather systems and you may have noticed that the earth itself is altering its vibrational energies and you have to realise that humanity plays a part in this. YOU play a part in this, because humanity, through its ignorance has created the changes, many of which are beginning to transpire in this of your lifetime.

You have to realise that you are all parts of each other, you're all parts of the same great whole and that what you do to others you do to yourselves. It is an absolute spiritual truth and fact that what you sow you will reap and you have a responsibility not only to yourselves but to the environment in which you dwell for a short time whilst in the physical body. Responsibility comes to you with spiritual growth. The more that you know, the greater the responsibility that you have and you cannot negate this. You cannot neglect it. You cannot put it aside and pretend that it doesn't exist and much of the trauma, pain and difficulty that humanity is today experiencing is the result of that which has been sown through successive generations before you. You may find that when you look around you, you see greater darkness, you see heartache, you see pain, you see those who should be liberated by the light of truth fighting to struggle against the cancer of oppression and you say 'what can I do to change it?'. You can begin to change it by changing yourselves. By looking within yourselves and allowing the divine aspect of the spirit which is inherent within all life to come to the surface. How do you do this? Well, first of all try to realise what you are. You are not merely flesh and bone. You are not the physical form that you see when you look in the mirror each morning. That is only an aspect through which your greater self is expressing itself. It is never total, it is only an aspect through which you come. You are neither male or female. You are beyond that, because you are of the spirit. But what is the spirit? What is God? Try to understand.....if I can put it in laymans terms, in simple language that you will understand, that you emerged from the Godhead like a tiny seed sent out upon the breath of life. You have no beginning or ending because the Great Spirit has no beginning and no ending but you have a 'commencement' upon this journey.

You come into form not at the top, not at the zenith, but somewhere at the bottom and you have to experience time and time again through successive vehicles, through successive forms in order to gain enrichment and enable the divine within you to unfold itself and to open up into the glorious flower of spiritual truth. Time and time again you come into form and each time when you come into human form you are within a different body. It may be male, it may be female. It may be that it is of the black skin, the white skin, the red skin or the yellow skin but underneath the spirit is beyond this. Every form that you come into has its own personality. You have your own personality that you think of as you. But it is not. The colour of your hair, the texture of your skin, your mannerisms, your height, your build, the tone of your voice, certain hereditary tendencies and predispositions which you have are the result of the genetic coding of your parentage which is given to you at birth. But you are beyond that. You are the individual that is beyond that, that comes into that body to experience through it. To touch upon this earth and to gain from it. That is the difference and you, in that time through your endeavours, through your service, can change so many things not only upon your own pathway but also the lives of those who come into your orbit. Because what you say and do, the way that you think and act has an effect upon the whole.

When you look out from your window at night and see the stars in the sky, you are looking at a part of yourself. You are not separate from anything.

When you look in the microscope or when you look into the river or the ocean you are looking at yourself. You are seeing reflected, a part of yourself and because you have the power of thought and action you can change so many things.

Service is the passport of the soul. Service is the coin of the spirit and when you serve, you are served. This is the way that the law operates. I do not want to paint a gloomy picture for you all because as I have said, when you look around you there are so many things which are of man's making which are having an impact now, here and in the future upon earth. Do not think that things are out of your control. As I have said so many times; if you want to change the whole, you have to change the sum total of its parts and your own individual life can make a great difference, depending upon how you live it.

Because you have the divine within you, there is no battle that cannot be won, no enemy that cannot be defeated, nothing over which you cannot eventually emerge victorious and I say to you this, as I have said many times; if you want to learn, then learn through everything that you experience. If you want to see, then close your eyes and look. If you want to listen, then shut your ears to the rantings and babblings of humanity, and listen. If you want to have movement then seek stillness. If you want to have stillness, then look at the movement that lies within it. Listen and look and observe everything. Look at the fool, he will teach you much. Look at the wise men, they will give you lessons which will help you along your pathway. Everything is your teacher. You are not separate from anyone. You are not greater or lesser than anyone or anything that is. Even your politicians and your royal families and your kings and your queens and your governments seem to think that they are above you and that they are there to be worshipped, there to be adhered to. That your men who wear their great robes of their religion and put themselves upon pedestals as spokesmen because they are 'people of God' must be listened to. No! You have God within you and you have greatness within you. Use it.

The only temple that you need is the temple of life itself. The only cathedral that you need is nature. The only great book is the book of life. You my friends are of the spirit. You and I, though we are different, we are the same. Although we are apart, we are together. Although we are each unique, we a part of the same spiritual family. May the Great Spirit bless you all."

White Feather has delivered his teachings to humanity for over twenty five years, speaking to many thousands of people from all walks of life in the process. He has faithfully answered every question put to him selflessly, truthfully and without a moment's hesitation.

All he has ever sought to do is to help disperse the mists of ignorance which prevent the light of truth from liberating humanity.

His is a labour of love, for he has sacrificed much in order to reach us here upon the earth, but if one sentence, one phrase or a single word found within these pages touches the heart and mind of its reader and awakens the divine potential within, then his efforts will have been justified.

There can never be a more glorious victory than that of truth over ignorance and no happier soul than the teacher from another world whose love and gracious presence has touched us all.

Epilogue

We hope that you will have found something of interest in this latest edition of White Feather teachings. For many, it will be further knowledge on which to ponder, enhancing subjects already discussed. For the uninitiated, we hope that the seed of curiosity for further exploration into the unseen world has been awakened.

It would be most unusual if everything you have read makes perfect sense or that you agree with all that has been written. These writings should be questioned. Asking whether your reasoning mind accepts the imparted philosophy, is important. These words are not meant to indoctrinate, to preach or to in any way channel your mind into believing a pre-set collection of rules and regulations that require robotic-like repetition.

Hopefully, they will inspire you as individuals to use your own intelligence and most powerfully the potential of your higher consciousness to make a positive contribution not only to your own earthly existence but to empower other souls to evolve to the greater echelons of spiritual development in the afterlife.

We believe that in offering the opportunity for people to look beyond the material and the biased views of those in thought-policing environments we can all move forward to a life where individuality is celebrated and the finer, delicate and humble attributes are welcomed, rather than the obscene hunger for material or monetary gain and the desire on the parts of many to fight ignorance with ignorance.

We will leave you with one last thought as we prepare for the next 'tour' - are you ready yet to look with the eyes of the spirit, speak the truthful words of the spirit and act in all good faith with the actions of the Great White Spirit?

If you are, friends, then you join us on a journey of change and development that can only direct us to a more fulfilling, humanitarian and loving world and one in which our children, our childrens' children and many generations to come can begin to reap the harvest from our carefully planted seeds.

Benediction

"You cannot be other than where you are.
Even if to your understanding and intellect at the moment
you think you are in the wrong place or at the wrong time,
you cannot be because the law operates with a
wondrous perfection that is never wrong,
and chance and luck and fate do not exist
in a universe that is regulated by perfect law.
So where you are now is where you are meant to be,
whether you like it or not, that is how it is.
Even though through your past deeds and actions
you have actually placed yourself in the place that you are now,
you will also determine the place that
you find yourself tomorrow and the day after
and a hundred and a thousand years from now.
That is why it is so important now to guide and to
guard your thoughts carefully, to think and to act in a way
that is concurrent with your spiritual understanding and awareness.
You have a responsibility to yourself to do that.
If you want to change something then act upon yourself
and upon your environment now, because you are sowing
the seeds of your tomorrow."

White Feather

You've read the book,
now visit the White Feather website!
http://web.ukonline.co.uk/mandrob

The web pages are updated on a regular basis,
so why not e-mail your philosophical question to White Feather
and we'll do our best to ask for a reply!

Please note that whilst we will do our utmost to respond to all
requests, replies are subject to our contact with the
spirit world and to the volume of enquiries at the time of writing.